# KNOT GARDENS

## ——— AND ———

# PARTERRES

# KNOT GARDENS

## — AND —

## PARTERRES

A HISTORY OF THE KNOT GARDEN AND
HOW TO MAKE ONE TODAY

ROBIN WHALLEY

ANNE JENNINGS

BARN ELMS

in association with the Museum of Garden History

DEDICATIONS

*To Karen Hiscock for her unfailing generosity*
*and constant support – Robin Whalley*

*To Rosemary Nicholson in thanks for her support*
*and the opportunities she has offered me. Also to the*
*memory of John Nicholson – Anne Jennings*

First published in 1998 by Barn Elms Publishing,
Flint House, 11 Chartfield Avenue, London SW15 6DT

Reprinted in 2000, 2006 and 2008

Printed in China by 1010 Printing International Limited
All rights reserved
Typeset in Palatino

Text copyright © 1998
Foreword: The Marchioness of Salisbury
Part One: Robin Whalley
Part Two: Anne Jennings

Photographic credits appear on page 160

Conceived and edited by Jane Crawley
Special photography and design by Jessica Smith

Robin Whalley and Anne Jennings are hereby identified as the
authors of this work in accordance with Section 77 of the
Copyright, Design and Patents Act 1998.

British Library Cataloguing in Publication Data. A catalogue
record of this book is available from the British Library.

ISBN 978 1 899531 04 1

The illustrations used on the front
endpapers and as the chapter title decorations
in Part One are from William Lawson's
*The Countrie Housewifes Garden*;
those on the back endpapers are from
*Maison Rustique*, and those used as the
chapter title decorations in Part Two
are from Thomas Hill's
*The Gardeners Labyrinth*.

*Title page.* The clipped garden at Ham House is
simple but effective all the year through.

# CONTENTS

FOREWORD

by The Marchioness of Salisbury

7

| PART ONE | PART TWO |
| --- | --- |
| by Robin Whalley | by Anne Jennings |
| A HISTORY OF THE KNOT GARDEN | HOW TO MAKE A KNOT GARDEN |

| | |
| --- | --- |
| PREFACE | ELEMENTS OF DESIGN |
| 13 | 97 |
| CHAPTER ONE | PLANTS FOR YOUR KNOT |
| UNRAVELLING THE KNOT | 111 |
| 15 | |
| CHAPTER TWO | DESIGNING YOUR KNOT |
| THE EARLY TUDOR PERIOD 1485 - 1558 | 140 |
| 27 | |
| CHAPTER THREE | MAKING A PLANTING PLAN |
| LATE TUDOR AND EARLY STUART 1558 - 1625 | 144 |
| 43 | |
| CHAPTER FOUR | PREPARING THE GROUND |
| FROM KNOTS TO PARTERRES 1625 - 1714 | 147 |
| 59 | |
| CHAPTER FIVE | FROM PAGE TO GROUND |
| REVIVALS AND RESTORATIONS AFTER 1800 | 151 |
| 77 | FUTURE CARE AND MAINTENANCE |
| | 154 |

KNOT GARDENS TO VISIT

156

BIBLIOGRAPHY

157

INDEX

158

Acknowledgements and Photographic Credits

160

# FOREWORD

*The Marchioness of Salisbury*

As a gardener who has lived the greater part of her life in Tudor, Elizabethan and Stuart houses and who therefore has a particular interest in and feeling for the gardens that would have surrounded them, it is a special pleasure for me to introduce this book. It is a work which many who have essayed to make a knot garden or a parterre will wish that they had had beside them when they were making their plans. There would then have been little need for all that intensive search and research, for here, enclosed in one cover, is most surely collected all that is known of the history and evolution of the knot garden and parterre. I certainly felt this and envy those planning their gardens after its publication, remembering the hours I spent delving through Thomas Hill's *The Gardeners Labyrinth* and other books of those times. Pleasant as those hours were (the charm of Hill's instructions and descriptions cannot fail to please), the gardens I was trying to design for the Tudor Palace at Hatfield would, I am sure, have been completed somewhat sooner if I had had Robin Whalley and Anne Jennings's book to study.

This is a work that has arrived at a most timely moment for there has been a retreat from the so-called 'landscaping' of gardens back to formality in the last years. The principle that the garden enclosed with walls or a hedge should be quite a different thing from the landscape outside it, and that the architecture of the house should dictate the architecture of the gardens surrounding it if the result were to be a harmonious relationship between the two, had been abandoned early in the eighteenth century. For those of us who admire and attempt to follow this principle the villain who started the rot was a man called Switzer. Gentlemen, he said, should remove their walls and fences and make twenty acres look to be two hundred or even three hundred. Woods and cornfields should be made to look as part of the garden. Those large sums of money buried within the limits of a high wall 'upon trifling and diminutive beauties of greens and flower' should be lightly spread over great and extensive parks and forests. Nature, he said, 'cashiers those Interlacings of Box-work, and such-like trifling Ornaments' in favour of natural and polite gardening.

Switzer was followed by William Kent who tried to reproduce the landscapes of Claude and Poussin. These efforts were described by Walpole. Kent 'leapt the fence', he said, 'and saw that all nature was a garden'. He too, brilliant architect and designer though he was, ignored the necessity for an architectural relationship between house and garden if satisfactory harmony was to be achieved. 'Capability' Brown followed and after him Repton. With them and the other exponents of the landscape school, the death knell of some of the finest formal gardens in Great Britain, large and small, was sounded. As Sir William Chambers said, 'Our virtuosi have scarcely left an acre of shade, or three trees growing in a line from Lands End to the Tweed', and Sir Walter Scott in a paper he wrote for the *Quarterly Review* pointed out the irreparable folly of destroying those formal gardens and the fallacy of claiming for

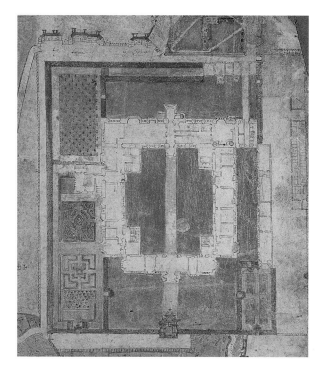

landscape gardening that it was loyal to nature. Of an old garden he noted in his journal for 29 August 1827: 'yew hedges, labyrinths, wildernesses, are all obliterated, following the new fashion, and the place is as common and vulgar as maybe'.

The great charm of the formal garden lay not only in its harmonious relationship with the house it surrounded, but in its contrast with the world beyond, whether simple farmyard, woods, hedgerows, cornfields and meadows or even a church and village. There would be a strong line of demarcation between the garden and the landscape outside, whether it were a fence, a wall or a bold and thick hedge of yew, holly or hornbeam. Within would be found the flower garden, with its walks and *allées*; the ornamental water, the fruit trees and the vegetables. It is

*Figure i previous page*. Lady Salisbury's planting of the East Garden at Hatfield House shows how bold informality can work superbly within the neat confines of box hedging.

*Figure ii above left*. A plan of about 1608 of the Old Palace from the archives at Hatfield House. Knot gardens were a feature then as they are now.

*Figure iii*. The knot garden at the Museum of Garden History in Lambeth was designed by Lady Salisbury. It is now cared for by Anne Jennings.

within an enclosed space, an *hortus conclusus*, that can happily be placed the knots and parterres whose history and construction are so eloquently described in this book.

For at least two and a half centuries the settings for houses and the houses themselves have suffered aesthetically from the rejection of formality in gardens, and until quite lately there has been small interest in formal gardening. Now, at last, there seems to be a change, indeed a veritable Renaissance has occurred as far as the rebirth of interest and admiration for the formal garden is concerned. Miles of box hedging are being sold; statuary and garden ornaments have to be alarmed or they are stolen to satisfy the demand for them; early orders for yew plants have to be made or they are sold out; nurseries specialising in topiary and box have appeared, and fountains, paving and cobbles are increasingly being used in the design of gardens. There is even a Topiary Society.

Within these newly designed formal gardens the knot and the parterre have their perfect setting. The knot being based on a square can be fitted into almost any space; it can be reduced or enlarged at will while a parterre can be designed to fit within the space available. Nor need it be a mere pastiche of a sixteenth or seventeenth-century knot or parterre. Both will lend themselves to modern interpretations. Indeed there are already signs that some of today's garden architects and designers, accepting the principle of the absolute need for architectural harmony between buildings and their surroundings plus the strict divorce between garden and landscape, are creating something new and exciting for the twenty-first century. In doing so they could resurrect the architectural beauty and peaceful atmosphere of those early gardens.

I understand such an atmosphere may be felt in the garden which I designed for the Museum of Garden History at Lambeth surrounding the tomb of the Tradescants, the famous sixteenth and seventeenth-century gardeners and plant hunters. It is here that Anne Jennings, the co-author of this book, presides as an imaginative and dedicated Head Gardener with a skilled team of volunteers.

Those architects and designers who read this book, indeed all those involved in the constructing and planting of knots and parterres, will find not only a great deal that is of historical interest, but also practical advice and encouragement on how to achieve their ambitions. To somewhat adapt Parkinson's words: 'By setting your knots and trayles you will therein find much delight'.

*Figure iv*. **A newel post at Hatfield, traditionally said to be of the gardener John Tradescant.**

# A HISTORY OF THE KNOT GARDEN

## ROBIN WHALLEY

1. Knot gardens at Hatfield House. As she explains in her Foreword
Lady Salisbury used sixteenth and early seventeenth-century
examples as the basis for her designs.

a Scale of 32: Foote

Heere I have made the true Lovers Knott
To tyit in Mariage was never my Lott.

# PREFACE

*'may please your fancy better than mine'*

It is easy to imagine that someone unfamiliar with the history of European gardens could be puzzled by the title of this book and ask what if anything knots have to do with gardens. Knots are generally thought of as useful and sometimes decorative features of everyday life – shoelaces, plaits and bows. However the experience of trying to undo a knot can be exasperating, and yet success in unravelling it can turn irritation into pleasure. The Spanish poet and writer Juan Eduardo Cirlot in his *Dictionary of Symbols* (English translation, 1962) wrote, 'To undo the knot was equivalent to finding the 'Centre' which forms such an important part of all mystic thought'. This introduces the notion that as well as being decorative knots have hidden qualities lying beneath their immediate practical use and transforming them into symbolic objects. It is the decorative and symbolic aspects of knots which are prominent in the history of knot gardens – the weaving together of living plants to make complex patterns on the ground – and it is these which are the subject of this book.

We have arranged the book in two parts. The first deals with the appearance of the knot motif in history and the development of knot gardens from their first mention to the present day. Although belonging historically to Tudor times, the knot garden slips seamlessly into the fashion for the parterre, which in turn had developed its full decorative potential by the end of the seventeenth century. The nineteenth and twentieth centuries revived old ideas and at the same time created new types of patterned gardens which have their own identity. More recently the enthusiasm for history and heritage has led to an upsurge in methodical restorations and some inspired recreations which have brought history and contemporary practice together.

The second part of the book is a practical guide exploring different ways of creating and using knots as a garden feature. Anne Jennings deals systematically with the process of design, linking this to historical precedent, before covering the basic aspects of laying out the garden with consideration of site, soil, planting and maintenance. Her aim is to provide a thorough understanding of the different processes in the hope that this knowledge will give satisfaction to gardeners who would like to have a go themselves at planning, planting and maintaining their own knot gardens. She has based much of this advice on her experience as the gardener at the Museum of Garden History, where Lady Salisbury designed an authentic knot as the key feature of the Museum's garden. However as Stephen Blake said of knot gardens in *The Compleat Gardeners Practice* in 1664, 'those that may be invented by your selfe...may please your fancy better than mine'.

2. Stephen Blake's 'True Lovers Knott' comes from his *Compleat Gardeners Practice* (1664). Rosemary Verey based her knot at Barnsley House (plate 140) on this design and Anne Jennings shows how it can be used today on pages 146-47.

# CHAPTER ONE

# UNRAVELLING THE KNOT

*'So let your dances be entwined'*

Even a superficial look at ancient civilisations shows that they had mastered how to knot things together to make essential structures. The German architect and historian, Gottfried Semper, writing on the origins of architecture, thought that weaving and pattern making came before the building of structures; he emphasised that the first constructed shelters were made out of timber lashed and knotted together using techniques already familiar from weaving fabrics. Once cords had been twisted together, whether they were made from strips of animal hide, hair, wool, or plant fibre, the complexities of the different configurations would be learnt and developed since they were so important to these early cultures. So it was that knotting and weaving, although both arose for very practical reasons, became recognised for their decorative qualities.

By classical times the archaeological record provides abundant evidence of these knotted motifs being copied in other materials. Greek ornament includes the widely found 'guilloche' pattern, which was derived from two strands of woven or plaited fibres. It appears especially in relief decoration, and later in Roman mosaics and paintings, to make borders and other decorative designs (plate 13). Later still it became a popular feature in the pattern books of architectural ornament and was commonly used in revivals of the classical style.

It seems highly probable that the symbolic use of knots to unite and bind together developed along with their practical and decorative uses, and there is plenty of evidence that the appearance of the knot as a symbol occurred far back in history. Interlaced snakes can be found as early as the third millennium BC in Sumerian stone carvings (plates 5 and 7). Then in the fourth century BC, Alexander the Great, during his conquest of the East, was told in the city of Gordium that whosoever

undid the legendary knot would rule the world; he cut it with his sword and ever since 'cutting the Gordian knot' has been taken to mean a bold and decisive act.

In classical Greek mythology knots assumed their great significance as symbols of union and particularly of marriage. The tryst between Venus, the goddess of love, and Mars, the god of war (in themselves opposing forces), was symbolised by Cupid tying a knot to bind them together (plate 3). Subsequently Vulcan, the god of fire, angered by the union, made a knotted net to trap the unsuspecting pair and succeeded in entangling the two in its meshes while they slept. The theme of the knot used here to entangle and imprison has another manifestation in the form of the labyrinth which is also familiar when it appears as the garden maze. This derives from the story in Greek mythology of Daedalus who built the famous labyrinth on Crete for King Minos. On his journeys Theseus enters the labyrinth and slays the Minotaur who has been devouring the maidens of Athens. He escapes with the help of Ariadne who had given him a ball of wool so that he could retrace his steps. Theseus's success was commemorated at Delos with an intricate weaving dance (a familiar theme in many traditional folk dances) symbolising the complex pattern of the labyrinth and delivery from the power of the Minotaur. Thus the labyrinth becomes a living dance and is often represented on coins, vases, and later in Roman mosaics. It continues to be an influential feature of the medieval period and some writers have claimed that it symbolises the Christian way of life, which may account for the number of floor labyrinths found in European cathedrals: Chartres is a good example (plate 8). It also becomes an important feature of many early European gardens.

Daedalus appears in Ben Jonson's masque *Pleasure Reconciled to Virtue* (1618) in a dance which entwines

3. Cupid ties the knot in Veronese's *Venus and Mars united by Love*, 1576-84. Detail from the painting in the Metropolitan Museum of Art, New York.

4. The sitter in this sixteenth-century portrait in the Royal Collection is clad in a sumptuous garment entirely decorated with an intricate knotted pattern. At one time she was thought to be Isabella d'Este (1474-1539), a leading patron of the arts in Renaissance Italy.

5 and 7. These carvings on Sumerian cylinder seals are examples of woven and knotted patterns dating from the third millennium BC.

8 *right.* The medieval floor labyrinth in the nave of Chartres cathedral.

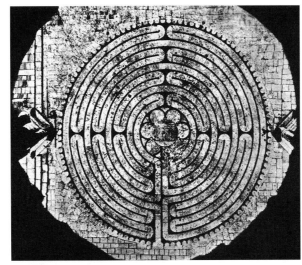

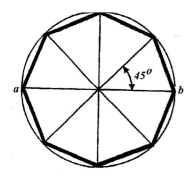

6. The octagon in a circle lies between the square and the circle – the symbolic geometric figures most often used in early knot garden designs.

This last reference is to the famous classical grouping of the Three Graces usually shown with their arms so enlaced as to weave their figures together. Given the notion of knots and mazes being so interwoven in the masque, it should come as no surprise to find that the formation of knots and mazes are treated as one and the same in the first gardening book, *The Gardeners Labyrinth,* printed in the age of Queen Elizabeth. It is significant too that such an enigmatic title should have been chosen for the first popular book on gardens.

The Greek god Hermes (the Roman god Mercury), messenger of the gods, is attributed with knowledge of knots and chains and symbolically carries the caduceus – a wand surmounted by wings, with around it a pair of interlaced serpents representing the balance between opposing forces: the spiritual and the material, heaven and earth. Snakes are often used to make a figure of eight which is also the Greek symbol for infinity; it is a key number with the octagon being an intermediate figure between the square and the circle (plate 6). Two squares can be superimposed on each other to make an eight pointed star, which is significantly a symbol of regeneration. It is no coincidence that the patterns for knot gardens which will be examined in the next chapter are all based on the square. Knot gardens constructed in the form of a square within a circle (see examples from Thomas Hill) could literally represent heaven on earth, and would again be a reference to the opposing forces. This would have been recognised, and understood by cultivated Elizabethans in particular, who, with their love of devices, enjoyed the emblematic nature of the knot and its different layers of meaning.

The symbol of the knot was readily transferred from one medium to another and is especially apparent in traditional clothes. The three knots in the girdle of the friar's habit represent the Trinity: Father, Son and Holy Ghost. Fishermen in the Shetlands believe they control the wind by the magic use of knot designs. Belts and buckles were also an important part of medieval dress and the clasp, appropriately, is often decorated with interlaced designs. Monograms of entwined letters are often embroidered on to a person's apparel, and other forms of interlaced designs form strong decorative elements, particularly on Tudor clothes (plates 4, 34, 60).

pleasure with virtue so that the two become indistinguishable, and also draws attention to the close connection between knots and garden labyrinths:

*Come on, come on: and where you go,*
*So interweave the curious Knot,*
*As ev'n the Observer scarce may know*
*Which Lines are Pleasures, and which not...*
*Then as all Actions of Mankind*
*Are but a Labyrinth or Maze:*
*So let your Dances be entwin'd,*
*Yet not perplex Men unto gaze:*
*But measur'd, and so numerous too,*
*As men may read each Act they do;*
*And when they see the Graces meet,*
*Admire the Wisdom of your Feet.*

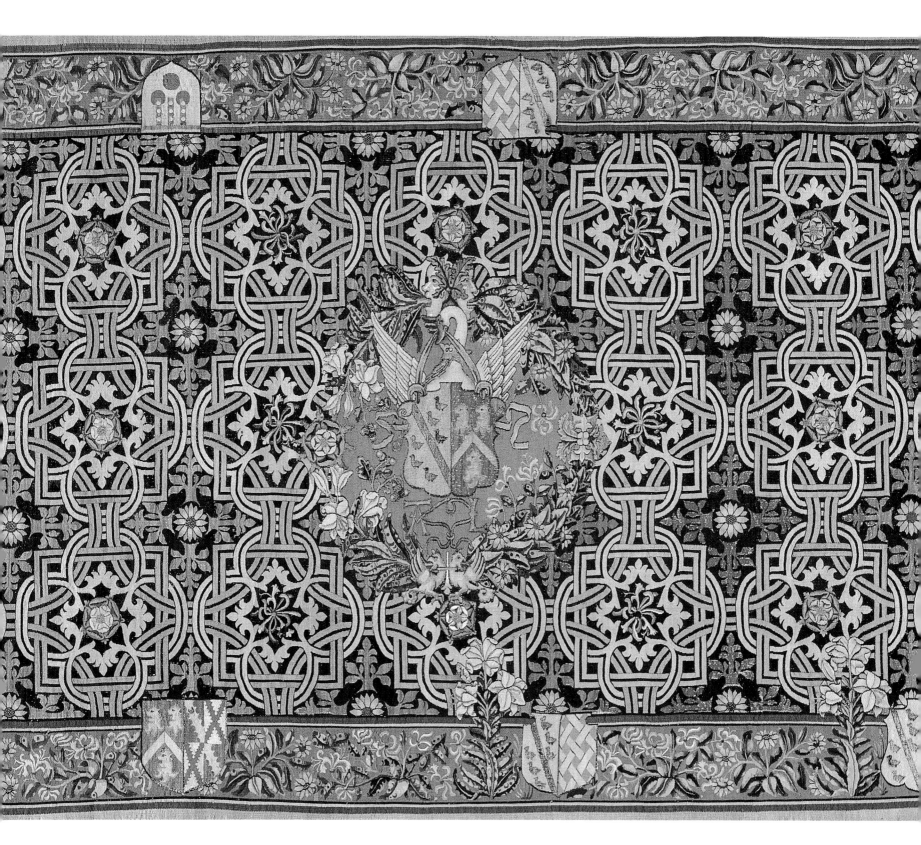

9 *left*. A section of the table carpet in the Burrell Collection, Glasgow, which was apparently woven for the widow of Sir Andrew Luttrell in about 1544. The interlocking design of squares, circles and quatrefoils could have been commissioned by Margaret Luttrell in memory of her husband and their marriage.

10. 'Carpet page' from the Lindisfarne Gospels (British Library) dating from the beginning of the eighth century. Similarities in the complex layout of interwoven knots make it look like a precedent for the Luttrell carpet. It is easy to imagine the Lindisfarne design as a garden with the knotwork on the paths providing a framework for the beds. The criss-cross designs which are positioned at the corners and sides outside the page's rectangle must be the basis for the criss-cross grid motif which appears in later examples of Christian art and which will also appear in Tudor embroidery.

Knotted designs were a key element in Celtic art and just as historians have looked for the earliest evidence of the knot garden, so they have looked for the first appearance of the knot motif in Celtic decoration and searched for precedents for this type of design. No significant examples of Celtic knots have been found among the archaeological remains of the Celtic regions of the British Isles and Ireland from before Christian culture spread northwards from Italy. The conversion of the Saxons by St Augustine from AD597 is a turning point in

the process of Christianisation in Britain which continued to spread in the following century; but according to the historian Romilly Allen surviving records show that up to AD650 there was no distinctive Christian art. What monuments there are from before this date show only the crudest forms of decoration.

In general decoration in early Christian art falls into the following categories: geometrical patterns, which are usually described as interlaced work, step patterns, key patterns, spirals and somewhat abstracted animal, human and botanical forms. The simple plait is the first to appear, and examples from the Romano-British

period have been found in this country, such as in the mosaics at Woodchester (plate 13). The spiral in particular was a strong motif in Iron Age decoration, and probably the only motif that was indigenous. It can be traced in pagan decoration whereas most of the other decorative elements can be compared directly with those of Italo-Byzantine origin. A study of the development of knotwork in Northern Italy shows an increasing elaboration during the Byzantine period in for example the decoration of the churches in Ravenna, seen here clearly in the pierced marble screen with its complex concentric design (plate 12). Is it a coincidence that this example is more reminiscent of the knot designs that appear in the sixteenth century than anything found in Celtic art (see plate 63)? However apart from this, work very similar to Byzantine 'circular knotwork' appears in northern Celtic manuscripts around AD700 and again, modified, in much later Celtic knot designs. This would suggest that knotwork in Britain during the early Christian period was in some ways close to its counterpart in Italy and that later it was evolving to some extent independently with Byzantine designs being adapted and changed.

It is in the manuscripts that some of the finest examples of Celtic art during the Christian period are found, and all the evidence from their decoration shows that the general form has great similarities to the style of Byzantine originals. Two of the most well known of the Celtic missals are the highly decorated Book of Kells (Trinity College Dublin) and the Lindisfarne Gospels (plate 10). The Lindisfarne Gospels have been dated around the beginning of the eighth century and the Book of Kells is probably about the same date. The Celtic decorative arts reached their most highly developed form in these manuscripts and it is this kind of interlaced decoration which appeared on other artefacts such as stone sculpture from the ninth to the eleventh centuries. The majority of these stone monuments are upright slabs or different kinds of crosses. Some crosses have a combination of spiral motifs, key patterns and interlaced work (plate 14), and these designs to some extent seem like pattern books for later knot designs, but there is in fact no evidence for any direct correspondence.

**11** *far left.* The Hunterston brooch in the Royal Museum, Edinburgh, is a very fine example of Celtic metal-work. It dates from the early eighth century AD and is silver-gilt with filigree ornament

**12** *above left.* An early ninth-century Italian pierced marble screen in Ravenna.

**13.** The mosaic floor at Woodchester, Gloucestershire (now permanently covered) is one of the richest sources of Roman mosaic ornament in the British Isles. The illustration shows a range of motifs including the guilloche pattern and a woven design which is strikingly like the very early Sumerian carvings.

**14** *right.* A Celtic cross still standing in Ahenny, Ireland. Such crosses are one of the most enduring symbols of their age and a rich source of Celtic ornament.

15 *left.* Dirck Bouts's medieval depiction of *The Justice of the Emperor Otto* (1468-75) shows a castle garden with a chequer board of five beds surrounded by low railings. Descriptions of Tudor gardens refer to such layouts and one can also compare the Gothic tracery in this painting with plans for knot gardens in William Lawson's *Countrie Housewifes Garden*, 1617 (plate 68).

16. Gothic figure painting is highly developed in the Lapworth Missal (1398) but around the illumination there is a border of tightly woven knots unmistakably derived from early Celtic patterns.

There has been much speculation as to how these intricate designs were worked out and it is believed that knotwork was developed first from the plait by introducing breaks at regular intervals. These designs then had to be transferred on to the manuscript page or the stone surface but there is very little indication as to how this was done. All the evidence seems to suggest that the process was based on a grid of squares that was applied temporarily to the surface with a pattern of pricks and that the points of articulation were then found on the diagonals and the points where the lines crossed. If this indeed was the process as described in Iain Bain's *Celtic Knotwork* (1986), it has a remarkable similarity to the very simple grid system which is recommended as the starting point for knot garden designs in the gardening books of the seventeenth century.

Highly decorated illuminated manuscripts were produced throughout the Middle Ages, and although the iconography was to change significantly as the Italo-Byzantine influence gradually weakened and the Gothic tradition strengthened during the twelfth and thirteenth centuries, there is a persistent use of knot-work decoration throughout this period. Most strikingly this is seen in the Glazier Psalter (Pierpont Morgan Library, New York), an English psalter of the thirteenth century, where the style of the figures generally reveals a northern Gothic form tinged with the ghosts of its Byzantine predecessors, but the knotwork decoration is extremely persistent and still owes much to the circular knotwork developed in Italy in the ninth century. Another example is the Lapworth Missal (plate 16), specifically dated 1398, showing a highly developed knowledge of Gothic figure painting, and skilfully stylised plants, woven into tightly knotted borders.

Practically all the evidence as to what medieval gardens looked like comes from illuminated manuscripts and the majority of these are Continental. It will be seen in the next chapter that there are no examples of knot patterns in the gardens depicted in manuscripts before those that appear in one of the earliest printed books, the *Hypnerotomachia Poliphili*. However two aspects of medieval gardens relate to the knot theme. In many illuminations a fence of wattles interwoven around stakes surrounds the garden (plate 19). As well as being practical this could allude to the mystical associations of knots as described by Cirlot: 'A knotted cord forms a kind of closed ring, or a circumference, and hence it possesses the general significance of an enclosure, and of protection' (*A Dictionary of Symbols*).

The illumination by Dirck Bouts shows a chequer board garden in the background within the walls of the castle (plate15). Some Tudor gardens are described as having this arrangement, but just as important is the prevailing idea of the 'square' which appears in so many medieval examples. It is the square which is the fundamental form of the knot and all the early illustrations of knot designs which will be discussed in later chapters are based on the square.

If one is fully to understand the knot garden in the Tudor period it should be studied alongside the history of the knot motif as an enduring symbol and evidence of an age which used and understood symbolism as part of daily life; it is in the later periods (after about 1650) when the knot is subsumed into the decorative notion of the parterre that consideration of the knot as a symbolic element in the context of the garden becomes increasingly irrelevant.

**17. This fine example of a knot design on a sixteenth-century leather binding shows that bookbinders were among those making use of the patterns from books such as Gedde's (plate 18).**

18 *above.* **Designs from Walter Gedde's** *Booke of Sundry Draughtes, Principally Serving for Glaziers: and not Impertinent for Plasterers and Gardiners besides Sundry Other Professions* **(1615).**

19 *above right.* **A sturdy woven wattle fence encloses and protects this medieval garden.**

20. **The labyrinthine knot has always fascinated and intrigued, but perhaps never more so than during the Renaissance. According to Vasari Leonardo da Vinci 'spent much time in making a regular design of a series of knots so that the cord may be traced from one end to the other, the whole filling a round space'. Leonardo's most famous knot, shown here in the engraved form, is a fitting Renaissance image to carry the knot from its early history in this chapter to its appearance in the garden in the next.**

21. The lunette by Giusto Utens of The Ambrogiana (1599) is a vivid record of an Italian Renaissance garden of the sixteenth century. It is laid out in squares and quarters, and one garden is divided from another by alleys and covered arbours, very like the gardens which appear later in this chapter (plates 30 and 32) and the next (plate 55).

# CHAPTER TWO

# THE EARLY TUDOR PERIOD
## 1485–1558

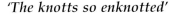

*'The knotts so enknotted'*

Although the knot motif emerges early on in history with a key role as a cultural and emblematic sign, there is no indication that it was used in garden making before the end of the Middle Ages, so the true quest for the knot garden in Britain begins in the Tudor period when the country entered a period of relative stability after the Wars of the Roses. Most books on the history of gardens include quotations from written sources which make reference to knot gardens in the early 1500s, but no image or detailed description is found in England until the second half of the century, so speculation as to how they were made and what they looked like remains extremely tentative. However, as will be seen, there is a set of late fifteenth-century woodcut illustrations from Italy which provides a unique source of information and it is generally assumed that the form of the knot garden in England could be derived from them. As they are both drawn and described in detail, they, together with later drawings purporting to show the layout of gardens of an earlier date, give us a fleeting glimpse of what the early Tudor gardens might have looked like.

The character of this period is shaped on the one hand by the traditions of chivalry and romance of the Middle Ages and on the other by the growth of humanism, learning, and education, springing directly from Renaissance Italy. This dichotomy can be seen in early Tudor buildings like Thornbury Castle, where, alongside such medieval features as fortified gateways and castellated walls, private apartments with canted bay windows, oriels and open galleries overlooked newly laid out gardens. Light in the new buildings literally pierced the gloom of dark Gothic interiors, and the larger windows allowed a new sense of pleasure in the natural world (plate 29).

The medieval garden, created in the Age of Chivalry and typically found within the castle or monastery walls, was to be transformed under the influence of the new learning. Precise knowledge about these gardens is limited and much of it gained from the study of illuminations and woodcuts. Taken together these illustrations demonstrate some of the essential characteristics of the medieval garden: the garden was usually small and enclosed by walls, palings or by a woven wattle fence, and the beds were usually rectangular and sited within trellis boundaries, and there were arbours and turf seats. Although the arrangement may be described as geometric, it does not conform to an overall concept of design and the siting of the garden appears to have no formal relation to the buildings. These gardens, like most medieval architecture, show an organic development responding to the immediate needs of defence, with the gardens conveniently and practically placed around the buildings. Renaissance ideas were to change this and two books appeared in fifteenth-century Italy which were to influence architecture and the shape of gardens throughout Europe in the sixteenth century.

The Italian architect Leon Battista Alberti completed *De Re Aedificatoria* in 1452 (it was published in 1485). For the development of architecture and gardens it was one of the most important books of the Renaissance, based on the rediscovery of classical literature. In it Alberti reveals his thoughts on buildings and gardens, relying especially on the writings of the Roman statesman, Pliny the Younger, and the Roman architect, Vitruvius. What, in Alberti's view, emerges, or is reborn, is that the architect must plan the villa along with its surroundings, and although he gives no prescription for garden design he develops broad principles: the garden must be planned in relation to the house, the garden must observe a geometrical framework like the house, and attention should be paid to enclosed gardens, using basic forms such as squares and circles, and include architectural topiary to enhance the shape. In his words: 'Let the Ground also be here and there thrown into those Figures that are most commended in the Platforms of Houses, Circles, Semi-circles, and the like, and surrounded with Laurels, Cedars, Junipers with their Branches intermixed, and twining one into the other'(Book IX, 4). His theory of symmetry and proportion could well be a prescription for the rules which appear later to govern the laying out of knot designs: 'So agreeable it is to Nature, that the Members on the right Side should exactly answer the left...that every Part...lie duly to the Level and Plumb-line, and be disposed with an exact Correspondence as to the Number, Form and Appearance; so that the Right may answer to the Left, the High to the Low, the Similar to the Similar, so as to form a correspondent Ornament in that Body whereof they are Parts' (Book IX, 7). This became a virtual dictum of design which was to apply to architecture and then to garden planning and was to alter gardens radically from the way they had been conceived in the Middle Ages.

The other book which encapsulated the spirit of the time and through its text and illustrations provides an unparalleled view of gardens in fifteenth-century Italy was the *Hypnerotomachia Poliphili,* written by the monk Francis Colonna in 1462, although not printed until some thirty years later in Venice in 1499. This book describes the romantic dream of Polyphilus as he searches for his love, Polia, and in it Colonna records in great detail the features of the gardens he travels through. It includes some 200 woodcuts of fantastic visions of ornamental structures and it is among these that gardens with knot patterns make their first appearance.

Colonna writes about four square knot designs with details of the plants used to make up the designs. The first has a border of pennyroyal and rue placed alternately to represent acanthus leaves, itself edged with marjoram and thyme interlaced together, and flowing into the 'embroidered' pattern in the centre. The knots so created are filled with red stocks, mallow, chamomile, rosemary, spring violets, pansies and four balls of hyssop, one at each corner. The second, a remarkable geometric pattern looking like lead glazing, is made with bands of white marble dust round the outside, and lavender, marjoram and tarragon to outline the pattern,

with marigolds in the spaces. The other two knots have heraldic birds at the centre, the one surrounded by a border with letters written in marjoram and edged with rue. It has a background of lily-of-the-valley, with the four outer circles of bugle, the inner circles with balls of myrtle on stems two feet high. The last design has the same knot, but outlined with different plants.

The first French edition of this book appeared in 1545, and then an English translation of the first half was published in 1592. The French edition would have been known in England during the second half of the sixteenth century, but none of the designs were copied or printed directly in English garden books of that period. However it becomes clear that the ideas of Alberti and the influence of such gardens as were depicted in the *Hypnerotomachia* spread northwards from Italy, through France to England during the late fifteenth and early sixteenth century. There were many

**23. Portrait of the Italian Renaissance architect Leon Battista Alberti (1404-72)**

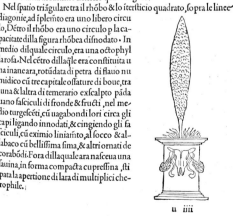

**25 and 26. Two more knots from the**
*Hypnerotomachia*. **One has an**
**emblematic bird at its centre made**
**from growing herbs. This idea of a**
**'living' emblem was to become a**
**central feature of Tudor knots. The**
**other geometric pattern looks so like**
**the glazing patterns used for example**
**at Little Moreton Hall (plate 43).**

**22 and 24** *left*. **Two pages from**
**Colonna's** *Hypnerotomachia Poliphili*
**(The Dream of Polyphilus) published**
**in Venice in 1499. One shows a**
**complex knot, the earliest to appear**
**in print. It is described in detail in**
**Colonna's text. The cypress tree**
**growing from an ornate pedestal is**
**a central feature of the knot.**

routes, but undoubtedly the French courts played the most important part.

The records show that when Charles VIII of France conducted his warring campaigns in Italy as far south as Naples in 1494 the gardens he saw inspired him to make new gardens in France. He brought back Italian craftsmen – one Pacello de Mercigliano was described as *'jardinier'*– and with their help the gardens of Amboise and Blois were then transformed, not least by Louis XII who succeeded Charles in 1498. Androuet du Cerceau's drawings in *Les Plus Excellents Bastiments de France* (1576) show the geometric layout of beds surrounded by a gallery, and although it is acknowledged that the knot patterns in the drawings may well reflect Du Cerceau's imagination more than reality (the illustrations were done some fifty years after the gardens were made), they are nevertheless a clear indication of the new form of the gardens (plates 30 and 33).

Francis I, an almost exact contemporary of Henry VIII, came to the throne in 1515 and embarked on the building of magnificent palaces and gardens which began to reflect the new humanist learning. He had developed strong links with Italy, particularly after his campaign to reestablish the French claim to Milan, and had invited the aged Leonardo da Vinci to come and live near his royal residence at Amboise. Although his intervention in Italy was to end in defeat in 1525 he maintained an Italian link through his queen's sister, Renée, who became the Duchess of Ferrara and sister-in-law to the young Ippolito d'Este. Francis I and Ippolito d'Este formed a lasting friendship, with Francis showering gifts on his Italian relative, and Ippolito becoming an important adviser to the French court until his death in 1572. Although the famous Villa d'Este, one of the most ambitious of Italian Renaissance gardens, was created after Francis I's death in 1547, it is nevertheless most likely that the two men would have discussed their plans for making new palaces and gardens. Francis I's rebuilding of Fontainebleau, which began in 1528 (almost parallel to the moment when Wolsey handed over Hampton Court to Henry VIII), is subsequently recorded in the drawings of Du Cerceau showing extensive gardens laid out beside enclosed courts overlooked by galleries. It was here also that the Italian architect

Sebastiano Serlio (1475–1554) came to work in 1540, after publishing the first ornamental parterre designs for gardens in 1537 (plate 31). It is speculation whether such books influenced the design of the gardens at Vallery, after 1548, where Jean d'Albion, whose father had been one of the governors of Francis's children, was to create one of the most sumptuous gardens in the new Renaissance style. The drawing by Du Cerceau shows a rich pattern of quartered squares, symmetrically arranged on either side of a long canal, and the whole rectangle enclosed on one side by a gallery and on the other by a wide raised walk to look down on the quarters of the garden (plate 33). Twin pavilions on either end of the gallery provide perfect Renaissance symmetry to the overall design as advocated by Alberti in his theory of proportion. Du Cerceau's drawings are invaluable for the study of sixteenth-century gardens and knots in particular. Sadly there is no other source to give us such a remarkable record, and in England there is only scanty information about gardens of this period.

Henry VII (1485–1509), with close family ties with the Burgundian courts, began to emulate their magnificence, and, in particular, his palace at Richmond seems to have been particularly influenced by them; it became famous for its timber galleries which were like the open loggias of Italian villas. At the time of the marriage of Prince Arthur in 1501 to Katharine of Aragon – the marriage which fulfilled Henry's dynastic ambitions for relations with Spain – the gardens of Richmond were referred to as 'his goodly gardeyns, lately rehersid, unto his galery upon the walles' (quoted in Kipling), and have been described in some detail:

under the King's windows, Queen's, and other estates, most fair and pleasant gardens, with royal knots alleyed and herbed; many marvellous beasts, as lions, dragons, and such other of divers kind, properly fashioned and carved in the ground, right well sanded, and compassed in with lead; with many vines, seeds and strange fruit, right goodly beset, kept and nourished with much labour and diligence. In the longer end of this garden beth pleasant galleries and houses of pleasure to disport in, at chess, tables, dice, cards, bills, bowling alleys, butts for archers and goodly tennis plays...' (quoted in Harvey, 1981)

Later drawings and paintings of Richmond show the gallery still in place, like the ones which were built to surround the palace gardens of Renaissance France. Clearly these sheltered galleries were constructed to look down on new gardens of intricate patterns and complex designs (plate 27).

Other written sources at the beginning of the new century provide the first mention of the making of garden knots. For instance the household account books for the old manor at Thornbury show a payment to the gardener John Wynde in 1502 for 'diligence in making knottes', and then at Alnwick in the same year a payment is recorded to 'attend hourly in the garden for setting of erbis, and clypping of knottes (quoted in Amherst), but most evocative of the new garden 'of pleasure' are the lines from a poem by Stephen Hawes, *Passetime of Pleasure, or The Historie of Graunde Amoure* (1509):

*Than in we wente to the gardyn gloryous*
*Lyke to a place of pleasure most solacyous.*
*With flora paynted and wrought curyously*
*In dyveres knottes, of mervaylous gretenes*
*Rampande lyons stoode up wonderfly*
*Made all of herbes with dulcet swetnes*
*With many dragons of mervaylous lykenes*
*Of dyvers floures made full craftely*
*By flora coloured with colours sundry.*

In 1510 the granting of a licence to Edward Stafford, 3rd Duke of Buckingham, by Henry VIII to impark land and fortify and crenellate his old manor at Thornbury was the start of an ambitious programme of building and the making of some of the finest gardens in early Tudor England. The building immediately displayed the contradictions of the period: a massive embattled and turreted medieval looking gateway led into a court-

27. In this seventeenth-century painting of Richmond Palace the outside of the timber galleries can be seen surrounding the Privy Garden. Galleries like these were constructed in Edward Stafford's garden at Thornbury Castle (*opposite*).

28 and 29. The privy garden at Thornbury Castle was overlooked by the private rooms of Edward Stafford, 3rd Duke of Buckingham, built between 1510 and 1521. The garden with its open galleries was the equal of that at Richmond Palace. The photograph below left is of a door handle at the castle bearing the Stafford knot.

yard bounded on the east by the Old Hall – a living space which echoed the communal life of earlier times – while to the south the duke's private rooms overlooked the privy garden in the second courtyard which was surrounded on three sides by open galleries. These covered alleys while providing a sheltered passage to the church were for viewing the gardens and should be compared with the galleries for the royal palace at Richmond (completed by 1501). The canted bay windows on the first floor of the private rooms would have looked down on the intricate layout of the knot gardens. The Stafford Account rolls describe the gardens as formal

with extensive use of herbs and some in the form of the heraldic Stafford knots which can still be seen carved on the Tudor doorways. John Leland in his *Itinerary* says the gatehouse was begun in 1511, but the castle was never completed; the planned magnificence of Thornbury quickly came to the attention of Henry VIII, who, wary of the demonstrative power of his courtiers, saw such houses as a threat to his position. The Duke of Buckingham was executed in 1521 on an alleged charge of treason.

Henry VIII came to the throne in 1509 as a young man of eighteen, and in the next twenty years he

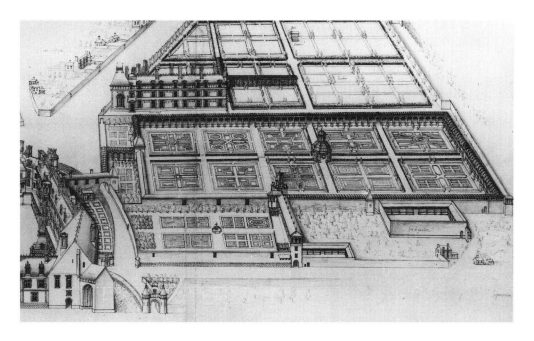

exhibited his power in pageants, fêtes, tournaments and jousting. In 1520 he arranged the most spectacular of all pageants on the Field of the Cloth of Gold. The great revelry in the Pas-de-Calais was to outdo his rival, Francis I, and it is such events that showed the close relationship between landscape and dominant power and how the gardens of Tudor England had their part to play in demonstrating royal supremacy.

Throughout this period magnificent gardens were made around the buildings and extensions of the royal palaces to emulate and outdo the finest royal gardens in France. Cardinal Wolsey was an exact contemporary of George d'Amboise, Archbishop of Rouen, who had accompanied Charles VIII on his campaigns. Like the king the archbishop was impressed with the arts and architecture of Italy. When he became cardinal in 1498 in Louis XII's reign he rebuilt the Chateau of Gaillon and was responsible for the great formal gardens created there between 1502 and 1506. Shortly after this Cardinal Wolsey, who one might surmise was trying to emulate the French garden at Hampton Court with gardens 'so enknotted, it cannot be exprest', set about enriching Hampton Court at the same time as Edward Stafford was building Thornbury. The building accounts for Hampton Court give us an idea of the size of the enterprise: the estate was over 2000 acres, and it was around the old manor that Wolsey began to lay out his gardens and orchards which were to impress his foreign visitors with new and ingenious knots to be compared with those in France. Unfortunately few descriptions of the gardens at this time survive and only the words of George Cavendish (1500–61), who wrote a life of his master, particularly describe the enclosed gardens and their knots. It is apparent from this memoir that the garden knots were surrounded by galleries such as the ones at Richmond and Thornbury and those illustrated in Du Cerceau's drawing of Vallery.

*My galleries ware fayer; both large and long*
*To walke in them whan that it lyked me beste;*
*My gardens sweet, enclosed with walles strong,*
*Enbanked with benches to sytt and take my rest:*
*The knotts so enknotted, it cannot be exprest,*
*With arbors and alyes so plesaunt and so dulce,*
*The pestylent ayers with flavors to repulse.*

Henry VIII was so impressed with Hampton Court that he took over the palace for himself in 1529 after Wolsey fell from grace. He then set about his own great and magnificent enlargements including the King's New Garden on the site of the present Privy Garden, which, as at Thornbury, was overlooked by the private apartments, and to which he took his young bride, Anne Boleyn, in 1533. The palace and its gardens must have had a special place in the hearts of Henry and Anne, for their monogram of interlaced letters appeared everywhere. One can imagine that, in keeping with the practice of making heraldic devices in the knots, H & A interlaced in a true lovers knot was set in herbs in the New Garden below their windows surrounded by the king's and queen's heraldic beasts.

One drawing by the Flemish artist Anthonis van Wyngaerde of about 1555 is our only surviving visual record of Hampton Court at that time showing something of the elaborate heraldry in the New Garden and the layout of the ground in squares and quarters. Although no contemporary descriptions of Henry's gardens survive, Thomas Platter, a Swiss nobleman travelling in England in 1599, gave an eyewitness account of his visit to what he describes as 'the finest and most magnificent royal edifice to be found in England, or for that matter in other countries':

By the entrance [to the garden] I noticed numerous patches where square cavities had been scooped, as for paving stones; some of these were filled with red brick-dust, some

30 *left*. This sixteenth-century drawing of the chateau of Blois by Androuet du Cerceau shows the early influence of Italian design.

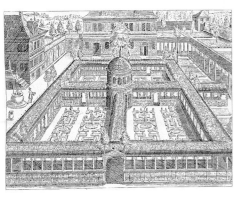

32 *above*. The Dutch artist Vredeman de Vries (1527-1606) was one of the first to publish garden designs in the sixteenth century. This example from *Hortorum Viridariorumque Elegantes* (1583) shows a garden with elaborate covered alleys or galleries very comparable to the ones in the garden of the Italian villa The Ambrogiana (plate 21).

31 *left*. Two engravings from Sebastiano Serlio's *Tutte l'Opere d'Architettura* (1537-47) show early comparisons between ceiling decoration and patterns for garden knots.

33. Androuet du Cerceau's drawing of the chateau at Vallery, symmetrically laid out following the principles laid down by Alberti and surrounded by arcaded galleries and a raised walk from which to view the pattern of intricate parterres.

with white sand, and some with green lawn, very much resembling a chess-board....There were all manner of shapes, men and women, half men and half horse, sirens, serving-maids with baskets, French lilies and delicate crenellations all round made from the dry twigs bound together and the aforesaid evergreen quick-set shrubs, or entirely of rosemary, all true to the life, and so cleverly and amusingly interwoven, mingled and grown together, trimmed and arranged picture-wise that their equal would be difficult to find. (from Platter; Williams, 1937)

Surely this is a description of topiary and most elaborate knot gardens, trained and intertwined, which no doubt had been planted and replanted over the intervening period of some seventy years. Some of Platter's account refers to those knot gardens where the spaces were filled in with coloured earths: in early Tudor days there were few autumn or winter flowering plants, so the use of coloured materials would have made up for this lack of natural colour during the winter months.

At the same time as Henry VIII took on Hampton Court he acquired Whitehall, previously called York Place, and again a former residence of Cardinal Wolsey. In 1529 he decided to make it another of his palaces and to have it ready for his marriage to Anne Boleyn. He greatly extended the gardens, again creating a privy garden overlooked by the king's chambers, and to the west of the palace the Great Garden, surrounded by an open gallery on the upper level. No description of the knots has come to light, but the arrangement of the beds surrounded by rails in the Tudor colours of green and white can be glimpsed through the open arches in the background of the painting of *The Family of Henry VIII* (plate 35).

The most magnificent and dazzling of all Henry's palaces was undoubtedly Nonsuch, and as only a few descriptions of the palace gardens have survived from the sixteenth century the wonders of its buildings and gardens are almost legendary, with the name itself implying something that cannot be surpassed. Leland in

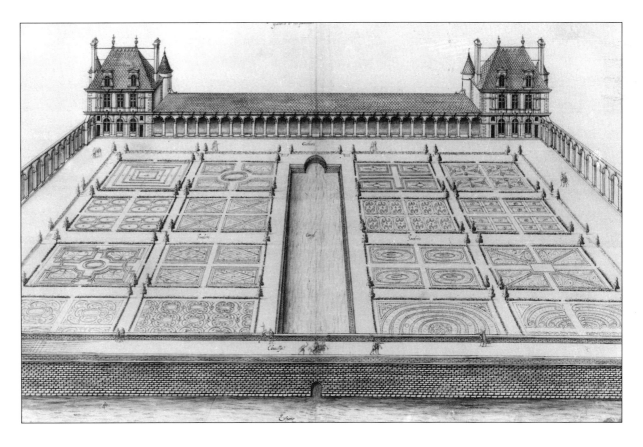

34 *left*. A portrait of Henry VIII attributed to Hans Eworth after Hans Holbein (probably 1560s). It is a marvellous example of Tudor costume and in particular shows embroidery on the hem of the cloak with knotted designs which compare directly with Thomas Hill's 'propre knot' (plate 51).

35. A detail from the painting of *The Family of Henry VIII at Whitehall* (*c*.1543-7) showing a glimpse of the Great Garden through the doorway with an arrangement of rectangular beds surrounded by heraldic rails painted in the Tudor colours of green and white.

his *Itinerary*, which was based on his travels between 1534 and 1543 when he found building in progress, was the first to register the wonders of Nonsuch, which were to inspire future travellers and writers, one of whom translated Leland's Latin verse as follows:

*This, which no equal has in art or fame,*
*Britons deservedly do Nonesuch name.*

Not surprisingly the palace became widely renowned in Europe for its splendour and for Henry became 'A Pearl of the Realm'. Unlike Hampton Court and Whitehall Palace, where existing buildings were remodelled and extended, Nonsuch and its gardens were all newly created between 1538 and 1547 on the site of a village in Surrey called Cuddington which had to be demolished to make way for the royal palace. How the gardens looked in Henry's day is an unanswered question, but it seems reasonable to assume from the surviving building accounts that when the Italian, Nicholas

Modena (who had worked with Francesco Primaticcio – one of the most influential Italian artists to work at Fontainebleau for Francis I) was employed in Henry's service from 1538, he brought with him knowledge of Italian and French architecture and that, although in overall appearance the building appears to be a fanciful medieval castle, the symmetry and decoration were beginning to reflect the new learning. The gardens and courtyards, certainly from inventories taken during Lord Lumley's tenure in the reign of Queen Elizabeth, displayed fine Renaissance fountains and antique statuary. From other evidence it appears many of the gardeners were Frenchmen who became 'denizens' in 1544 and were known to have been in the service of Henry VIII. This, together with the knowledge that French kings had imported Italian taste to make the gardens at Amboise, Blois and Fontainebleau, shows that Henry was developing the new taste at Nonsuch to outdo his rival in France.

**37** *right*. One of the very few visual records of Nonsuch is a vignette on Speed's map of Surrey (1610) where it is possible to discern a simple pattern of knots in front of the palace.

**36.** Anthonis van Wyngaerde's drawing of Hampton Court of about 1555 showing a view of the New Garden laid out with heraldic beasts and squares separated by alleys.

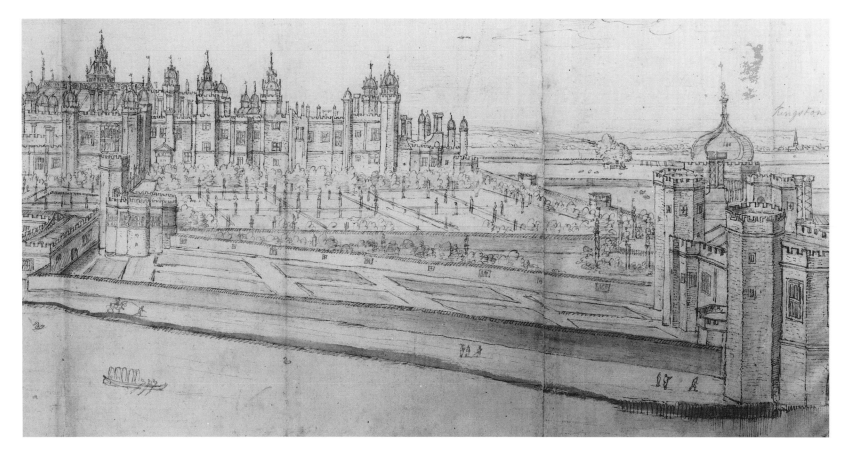

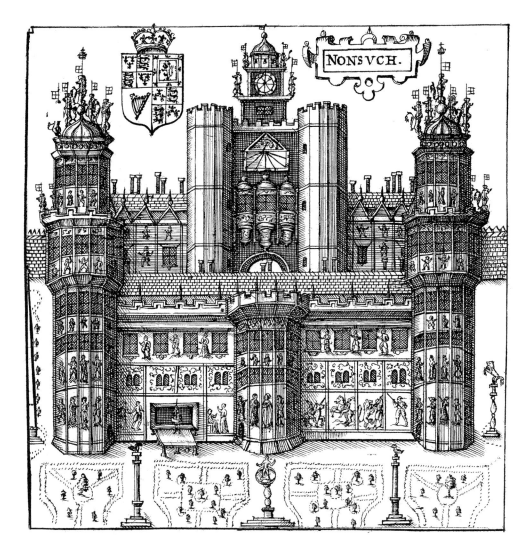

38. This little detail from sixteenth-century carved panelling at Haddon Hall, Derbyshire, shows knots interlaced with initial letters. Such devices would have featured in the knot garden.

and the pleasure gardens where there are 'charming terraces and all kinds of animals – dogs, hares, all overgrown with plants, most artfully set out, so that from a distance one would take them for real ones'. This last description must refer to topiaried heraldic beasts set out in and around the knotted patterns.

Although Nonsuch stood until its demolition in 1682/83, only a few visual records have survived; one is a vignette on Speed's map of Surrey, which shows the pattern of beds indicated before the south front of the palace, and although the drawing is extremely sketchy it does provide the outline of knot gardens, most probably dating from Lord Lumley's innovations in the garden in about 1580 (plate 37). Not long before Nonsuch was demolished a detailed survey of the house and park was completed in 1650; as well as describing the marble fountains in the Inner Court, it gives details of the layout of the privy garden with 'severall allyes quarters and rounds set about with thorne hedges all which though for the present in a condicion of some neglect' (quoted in Dent). This is the garden immediately to the east of the palace and clearly here are the remains of intricate knots dating from the early Tudor period.

Although we have to wait for the publication of Thomas Hill's *The Proffitable Arte of Gardening* in 1568 for our first indication of how knot gardens were to be made and what form they might take, there is evidence of possible garden motifs from other aspects of the decorative arts in the early Tudor period. Much has been made in recent books of the embroidery patterns, so often drawn from plant forms, and how these were either transformed into garden devices or used in pattern books to make more complex knots. Once it is evident how often patterns were successfully used in different materials, whether embroidered in fabric, pressed into leather, carved in stone, drawn on ceramic objects, used for glazing patterns in windows or woven into carpets, it is easy to see how these designs could have been transformed into a living tradition constructed with clipped herbs and other plants to give a significant form to the garden.

Other accounts of the Nonsuch gardens are provided by later Elizabethan writers and travellers. William Camden was one of the earliest to comment in his *Britannia* (first published in 1586): 'such dainty gardens and delicate orchards it hath, such groves adorned with curious Arbors, so pretty quarters, beds and Alleys'. This fragment along with Anthony Watson's more extensive writing towards the end of the century on the house and the overall documentation of the estate makes us very well aware of the scale of the gardens, and no doubt the 'pretty quarters' were filled with knots. Paul Hentzner, a German nobleman, records in 1598, 'delicious gardens... cabinets of verdure...a place pitched upon Pleasure herself', and a year later Thomas Platter gives a vivid description of his audience with Queen Elizabeth and then takes a tour of the gardens where he encounters the 'grove of Diana', a labyrinth,

Before the Elizabethan period there is very little indication in surviving documents about which plants were actually used to make the designs, and attempts to find an answer are based on a wide variety of literary sources. As box is so widely used today in the making of knot gardens, in spite of the controversy which surrounds the authenticity of this approach, it is worth giving this plant particular attention. The Romans used clipped box for topiary and hedges in the peristyle gardens of Italy, while the excavations at Pompeii have shown that the gardens there were essentially green gardens and that box was probably used for outline edging. Certainly Pliny provides a very clear example of this at his Tuscan villa where he speaks of 'the beds edged with box' and 'the rows of box in the form of animals facing each other' and of box cut into the shape of letters which spelt out names. As regards Britain, some botanists have doubts whether box was native to Britain at all as there is no box apparent in the fossil record, but archaeological investigation has recorded box at several British Roman sites, and it is possible that the Romans introduced box into their villa gardens. In *Early Nurserymen* (1974) John Harvey includes box in a list of plants cultivated in England between 1375 and 1400, relying on references to it in Chaucer.

During the Renaissance the first garden knots appeared in the *Hypnerotomachia* and were made with all kinds of plants other than box. If this is typical of figured gardens at this time the conclusion must be that box had fallen out of favour since the Roman period. Claudia Lazzaro would confirm this as she found little evidence for the general use of box for making patterns in villa gardens of the sixteenth century: 'One of the principal misconceptions about Italian Renaissance gardens concerns the use of box (*Buxus sempervirens*), which was a staple of the garden, but had only limited use alone as a low hedge.... The designs in the beds of the garden, as we shall see, were never created out of clipped box'. (*The Italian Renaissance Garden,* 1990).

In *De Re Aedificatoria* Alberti had recommended the planting of box to enclose walks, but also suggested using box 'to trace their...Names...in Parterres'. At the same time in Britain box is hardly mentioned; one of the earliest books to do so is William Turner's *The Names of Herbes* (1548), although this is not evidence in itself that box was being used or cultivated in this country as he merely draws attention to the origin of the name: in Greek – *Pyxos* from which we derive *Buxus*. Throughout the second half of the sixteenth century box often comes in for scathing criticism. Henry Lyte's herbal of 1578 countenances extreme suspicion for the properties of box and goes so far as to say that it is 'very hurtful for the brayne when it is but smelled to', and John Gerard in his famous herbal (1597) is equally condemning calling the smell 'evil and lothsome'. No herbalist or garden

39. A cushion cover at Hardwick Hall, Derbyshire, believed to be the work of Mary Queen of Scots, showing her cipher of a thistle and roses. The embroidered design looks as if it could have been taken straight from a garden.

40. Tudor Garden, Southampton. This was designed to show the plants and features of a garden in the sixteenth and early seventeenth century and embraces ideas which run through this chapter and the next.

writer of the time refers to box as a useful plant in the herb garden and box is never recommended for the making of knots before 1600.

Can it be established what knot patterns were made from in the early part of the sixteenth century? Again one can look back to the *Hypnerotomachia* where there is a very clear description of all the plants used to make the designs; they included marjoram, thyme, southernwood, lemon balm, hyssop, lavender, rue and myrtle. What mention there is of knots up to 1558, assumes that these kinds of herbs were used, and this is borne out by the plants referred to by Thomas Hill and other writers in the second half of the century as we shall see in the following chapter.

*Buxus.*
The Box tree.

**42** *above right*. **The woodcut from Gerard's** *Herball*, **1597, illustrating** *Buxus sempervirens*. **There is no mention of its use in knot gardens.**

**41 and 43** *below*. **The elaborate glazing patterns and decorative timber framing of Little Moreton Hall are echoed in the intricate patterns of its knot garden (see plates 87 and 88).**

**44** *opposite left*. **Sixteenth-century glazing patterns (from M. Jourdain,** *English Decoration and Furniture*, **1924).**

**45** *opposite*. **Knole, Kent. The staircase is a splendid example of strapwork, ceiling mouldings and glazing patterns which include motifs which were often used in knot garden design and can be found in such pattern books as Gedde (plate 18).**

Little Moreton
Hall Cheshire

# CHAPTER THREE

# LATE TUDOR AND EARLY STUART
## 1 5 5 8 - 1 6 2 5

*'New garments and imbroadery for the earth'*

Thomas Hill, who lived from around 1529 to about 1575, is essential for any understanding of the English knot garden in the second half of the sixteenth century; his position cannot be stressed enough. Despite this, very little is known about the man and attention to his work on garden knots has so far been summary and tentative. He is regarded as publishing the first garden book in England to include knot designs and certainly on available evidence no knot patterns were published before this. It is only possible to surmise from where he gleaned his all important examples.

The fullest account of Thomas Hill's life was published in the *Huntington Library Quarterly* in 1944 and opened with these words: 'During the first half of Queen Elizabeth's reign no one was more diligent in compiling and publishing handbooks of useful learning than a London citizen named Thomas Hill.... He was the active leader in expounding the mysteries of science in simple terms for unlearned laymen'. Thomas Hill describes himself as a Londoner on the title-page of his first gardening book *A Most Briefe and Pleasaunt Treatyse, Teachynge How to Dresse, Sowe, and Set a Garden*, which is undated but published about 1558. The work was republished in 1568 with a new title, *The Proffitable Arte of Gardening* and included a woodcut portrait of the author at the age of twenty-eight. From changes to this woodcut in later editions it has been possible to work out the approximate date of his birth and, although we do not know exactly when he died, his friend Henry Dethicke wrote a prefatory note to the first edition of *The Gardeners Labyrinth* (1577) referring to the recent interment of his friend, which seems to indicate that he died around 1575. These dates are critical in any attempt to find the sources from which Hill might have taken the patterns for his knot designs.

Hill published a wide range of books in his lifetime,

all of a more or less scientific nature. They are listed in *The Proffitable Arte of Gardening* (1568), and a further list appeared in *The Contemplation of Mankinde* (1571). Apart from this last title and the garden books, his publications included a work on physiognomy (1556), the interpretation of dreams (1559), a treatise entitled 'Natural and Artificiall conclusions' (magic), a book on the rare secrets of lakes and wells and the effects of lightning, two or three almanacs with prognostications, books on medicine, which included a treatment for the plague, astronomical treatises, and palmistry.

With such a wide range of subjects one has the impression that he was a populariser of science, marketing his work to make money from his ventures by giving advice to people in an age groping uneasily for scientific solutions. He was undoubtedly successful in his lifetime and editions of his works went on being published well into the seventeenth century. *The Gardeners Labyrinth* was one of the most popular with one of the last reprints in 1660.

In his gardening works Hill constantly acknowledges his debt to classical authors and quite correctly claims that his approach to setting a garden was supported by writers such as Columella, Varro, Pliny and many others whom he listed at the beginning. This would have appealed to aspiring learned Elizabethans, but as far as is known he contributed no original material from direct experience of horticulture and does not appear to be an expert on the subject of his publications. Nevertheless his works stand out as extremely competent when compared with the flood of cheap English handbooks on popular science.

With this impression of Thomas Hill what can be gleaned about knot gardens in the Elizabethan period? In Hill's first publication, *A Most Briefe and Pleasaunt Treatyse*, the title-page includes the significant and

46. Red Lodge in Bristol is a small town house of the period, built on the estate of a wealthy merchant in 1590. The knot garden has been constructed in an ideal position for looking down on from the upper floors. Appropriately the design has been taken from the ceiling mouldings in one of the bedrooms. It is an Elizabethan design, transferred to the garden to make a living geometric pattern correctly planned in a square. For ease of maintenance box has been used to pick out the figure, whereas Hill would have advised the use of germander, hyssop or winter savory.

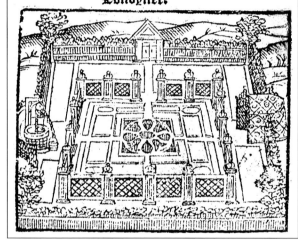

**47. The title-page from** *A Most Briefe and Pleasaunt Treatyse* **(first published about 1558) showing a small mid sixteenth-century garden, not unlike the one at Winchester House which appears on a London map of about 1553 (plate 50).**

extraordinary image (plate 47) which was to appear in his later works and their many editions. Extraordinary because it is the first image printed in England from a bird's-eye view showing what we must assume, although it is very stylised, is a typical arrangement of a mid sixteenth-century Tudor garden. It is a uniquely important record which we should fall on with delight as if we had recovered a precious jewel. Clearly a 'knot pattern' is the centre-piece of a square garden, made within an inner trellis fence, the whole being symmetrical from our view. The pedimented entrance to the garden is on the central axis, dividing it into two equal halves with the exception that a well on the left is balanced with an arbour on the right. The importance of this overall arrangement is that it shows how Alberti's principal ideas of the humanist garden had already

been incorporated, and although the use of trellis fences might be medieval in origin, the layout of the garden as a whole has adopted Renaissance principles of symmetry. Although in the last chapter it was seen how Italy and France had influenced the gardens at Hampton Court and Nonsuch with galleries and fountains, the dominating rules of architectural design, which appeared in late Elizabethan architecture with the work of Smythson and pre-eminently with Inigo Jones at the beginning of the sixteenth century, had not become apparent by the date of Hill's published woodcut. Perhaps too great a claim is being made for this design, which after all is taken to be an imaginary garden, but it is revealing to compare this image with the garden of Winchester House near Moorgate which appears in a 'Copperplate' map of about 1553 (plate 50). The map very clearly shows a square garden based on a central Italian looking fountain with a knot pattern around it, which is not unlike the one on Hill's title-page. The garden was owned by Sir William Paulet, Marquis of Winchester, and a leading statesman throughout the early Tudor period. Hill might well have known of it.

Hill's imaginary garden is the first printed English knot forming the focus of a garden layout and made by a pattern of beds shaped with an alternate arrangement of stylised flowers and hearts. Strangely there is only one mention of garden knots in this book, and this in the context of two images of the maze, both drawn in a square (in the 1568 edition one is based on a square and the other on a circle), and both appear repeatedly in subsequent works (plate 49). Providing these are not visualised with the preconception of the later tall hedge mazes, the connection between the knot and the maze is clarified by Hill's description of the second maze:

And here I also place the other maze, whiche may be lyke ordred and used, as I spake before, and it may eyther be set with Isope and Tyme, or winter Savery and tyme. For these do well endure, all the winter through grene. And there be some, whiche set their Mazes with Lavender Cotton, Spike [spike lavender], Maierome, and such lyke. For that mazes and knots aptly made do much set forth a garden, which nevertheless I refer to your discretion, for that not all persons be of like hability.

**48. A portrait of Thomas Hill. It was included in a number of his books.**

**49. These two maze designs were first published in** *A Most Briefe and Pleasaunt Treatyse* **before any knot gardens were included. They were often reprinted in Hill's later titles.**

Of the first Maze. Chap. v.

50a and b. These details of the 'Copperplate' map of London (about 1553) clearly show Winchester House with its unique garden arranged in quarters around a central Italian looking fountain. Winchester House was the town house of Sir William Paulet, Marquis of Winchester, a leading statesman throughout the early Tudor period.

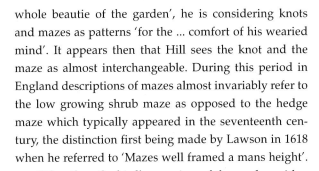

From this, the pattern of the maze can be visualised laid out on the ground with hyssop or thyme, no more than say twelve inches high. The knot and other Elizabethan devices are symbolic forms, a way of presenting Tudor conceits: the meaning has to be discovered or decoded, and the maze solved by arriving at the centre and being in possession of knowledge. Is it significant that in the first maze the man at the centre holds a spade representing the gardener, who presumably has found the secret of gardening, and in the second the figure is a gentleman with a sword, perhaps representing the owner of the garden, who now equally holds the secret? Thomas Hill gives no explanation of this and indeed none of his gardening books make any reference to the symbolism of knots or their use as conceits in the garden, but in his description of the maze Hill refers to mazes and knots together, as a necessary asset in a garden. Later, in *The Gardeners Labyrinth* (first published 1577), when he writes of covered alleys with 'windowes properly made towardes the garden, whereby they might the more fully view, and have delight of the

whole beautie of the garden', he is considering knots and mazes as patterns 'for the ... comfort of his wearied mind'. It appears then that Hill sees the knot and the maze as almost interchangeable. During this period in England descriptions of mazes almost invariably refer to the low growing shrub maze as opposed to the hedge maze which typically appeared in the seventeenth century, the distinction first being made by Lawson in 1618 when he referred to 'Mazes well framed a mans height'.

Other than the bird's-eye view of the garden with a knot in the centre, the first 'propre knot' appears in Hill's *The Proffitable Arte of Gardening* (1568). However the knot is not described or referred to in any of the chapters although it is given the following caption: 'A propre knot for a Garden, where as is spare rowme enough, the whiche may be set either with Tyme, or Isop, at the discretion of the Gardener'. This knot, like the title-page we discussed earlier, has a unique position among the knot designs that will be looked at presently. Unlike the designs which appear in the later editions of *The Proffitable Arte* and *The Gardeners Labyrinth*, which are derived from more obvious geometric patterns, drawn perhaps with compass and line with a degree of precision, this knot (plate 51) is made of flowing lines as if from a calligrapher's pen, or taken from the golden threadwork of the embroiderers' art as seen on the hem of Henry VIII's short cloak (plate 34, especially compare the designs in the four corners of Hill's knot with the design on the hem). It could therefore have been copied from an embroiderer's pattern book – embroidery very similar to knot garden designs can be seen on the prayer book for Katherine Parr, sixth wife of Henry VIII, embroidered by the Princess Elizabeth in about 1544 when she was eleven years old (plate 54). In Hill's 'propre knot' notice in particular that the four separate flower shapes around the central ellipse and the four imposed fleurs-de-lis at the top and the bottom suggest *appliqué* design. As a drawing for reproduction it would have been difficult to cut the block to leave such thin lines in place (for the lines are the only raised area of the block). This would suggest that the engraver was actually copying from threadwork. How does one imagine the design was transferred on to the ground with thyme and hyssop? Although the lines intersect there is no indication

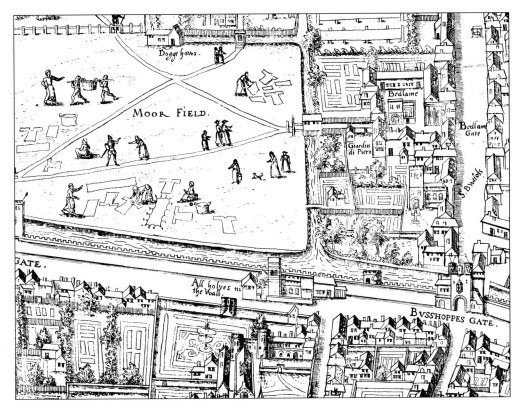

of weaving (as in later knots) and if the double lines are interpreted as a ribbon of vegetation, then the design has to be taken as a kind of template (in other words different designs could be copied from it) rather than one complete design, which may be what is implied by 'spare rowme enough'.

It has been suggested that the design could have been derived from Du Cerceau's engravings, of such gardens as Blois or Vallery (plates 30 and 33). The date of publication would make this impossible as Du Cerceau's *Les Plus Excellents Bastiments de France* was not published until 1576, and it would appear highly unlikely that Hill had access to Du Cerceau's unpublished drawings of an earlier date. In her *Old English Gardening Books* E.S.Rohde quite rightly draws comparisons between Du Cerceau's engravings and Hill's for maze designs and suggests that they may both have

Place this knot in fol. 189.

A propre knot for a Garden, where as is spare rowme enough, the whiche may be set either with Tyme, or Isope, at the discretion of the Gardener.

51. The first 'propre knot' appeared in Hill's *The Proffitable Arte of Gardening* (1568). It is a design which could so easily have been taken from a pattern book for embroidery.

52. Red Lodge, Bristol. A view looking down from the house. The knot garden was designed in the late 1980s with Tudor examples in mind.

53 *right*. Hovenden's map of All Souls, Oxford (about 1590) shows an elaborate garden of contemporary knots. One at least is very similar to the designs which were printed in *The Gardeners Labyrinth* (plate 58).

54 *opposite bottom left*. When she was eleven years old Princess Elizabeth embroidered the cover of this prayer book for Katherine Parr. It is evident that such knotted designs were used as much in embroidery as in gardens.

55 *far right*. There has been much speculation about the whereabouts of the garden depicted in this portrait of Sir George Delves and his wife dated 1577. It shows an elaborate sixteenth-century layout, including tunnel arbours (or galleries) surrounding different square compartments, one with a maze and another laid out in quarters around a candelabra type fountain. Examples of these kinds of galleries can be seen in the Utens painting of The Ambrogiana (plate 21), the engraving of a garden by De Vries (plate 32) and the Androuet de Cerceau drawing of Blois and to some extent of Vallery (plates 30 and 33).

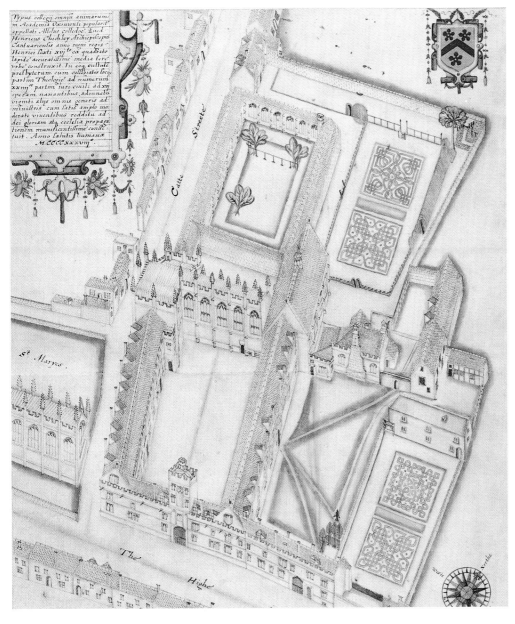

both mazes appear again among the illustrations. However there are additional chapters and five new wood engravings of garden scenes (plate 69), and – most important – twelve new knot designs in addition to the 'propre knot' which was discussed above and now has a new caption: 'A propre knot to be cast in the quarters of a garden, or drawn as there is sufficient room'.

Hill offers no other instruction or advice on the planting of knots, but for the maze, or 'delectable labyrinth' as he now calls it, his proposal is almost the same as before – plant 'with Isop and Time, or the Winter Saverie onely'. His intentions for the knot garden would not have changed.

The twelve new designs in the first edition of *The Gardeners Labyrinth* are all on the square with more or

been copied from 'some well-known original'. This seems very likely as Hill's round maze, for example, shares great similarities with the medieval floor mazes at both Chartres Cathedral (plate 8), which survives, and the one at Rheims Cathedral constructed in 1240 but destroyed in 1779.

The next printed knots to appear in Elizabethan England were in Hill's last publication, *The Gardeners Labyrinth* (1577, published under the pseudonym, Didymus Mountain). It was probably the finest gardening book published in England before the end of the sixteenth century. The text is not the same as *The Proffitable Arte*, although for example in dealing with aspects of 'setting a garden' his advice is markedly similar and less geometric patterns, all with symmetrical quarters, and all traced with parallel lines which represent the vegetative pattern. As they are double lines it is possible, as has been done, to indicate how the ribbons of vegetation weave together. Only one has straight lines throughout, all the others have curves in one form or another. At least four of the designs have a grid-like weaving pattern, some are made with just two interweaving patterns, and one with as many as five. One is set within a circle with four 'fleurs-de-lis' at the corners, but it is not clear what Hill's intention would be for plants to pick out these four shapes (they look more like designs for cut turf which appeared much later in the seventeenth century). None of the patterns offer a way in and one presumes the design of the ribbons is all important and that there is no planting within the spaces (much later such designs are referred to as 'closed knots'). All are very different from the single line 'propre knot' which appears in this and Hill's earlier books. One of these twelve designs (plate 58) may well have been the source for the new garden at All Souls, Oxford, about 1590 which is shown in Hovenden's map of the college which is contemporary with the making of the garden (plate 53). Thomas Trevelyon, a writing-master in London, was to copy one of these designs 'For Joyners, and Gardeners' into his 'Miscellany' of designs (1616), thus showing how general it was to share the same designs in different trades and crafts.

It is in this book that Henry Dethicke, who wrote the dedication to *The Gardeners Labyrinth*, refers to his friend Thomas Hill as 'lately interred', and one wonders at what stage in the preparation of the book the knots were included. No obvious source has yet been found for these designs and although the first French edition of *Maison Rustique* appeared in 1570 (see following page), with much useful information on the laying out of the parterre, it did not include any illustrated designs. No other published source up to this date shows knot designs (with the exception of Serlio's parterre designs, published in Venice in 1537, and those in the *Hypnerotomachia*). Hill's designs differ significantly from nearly all the others published towards the end of the century by virtue of the fact that no shading of any kind has been included (later designs are given a three-

56. This 'propre knot' appears in the 1594 edition of *The Gardeners Labyrinth* replacing the earlier one (plate 51), but it had already been printed in *Maison Rustique* which shows the steady influence of this French book of husbandry.

dimensional appearance through shading). This again suggests they could well have been traced from embroidery patterns of the time or worked up from glaziers' or carpenters' pattern books.

*The Gardeners Labyrinth* became a popular book and continued to be republished for almost the next hundred years with very little change to contents or illustrations. Significantly the unique embroiderers' 'propre knot' which had appeared in all Thomas Hill's garden books to date was dropped from the 1594 edition and replaced by an elaborate knot (plate 56) although the caption quoted above was not changed. This knot had first appeared in *Maison Rustique* in 1586, the first edition to include illustrations for parterres, and featured in many subsequent editions. It is made up of a central square knot pattern, surrounded by a border of knot designs. From the present consideration the shading used in the knotted design gives this image a three-dimensional aspect missing from Hill's earlier knot patterns (1577). The border looks like strapwork such as can be seen in the woodwork surrounding the Great Staircase at Knole (plate 45). Virtually no changes were made in the next edition, but by the mid seventeenth century (1652) the knot designs had been completely changed as will be described in the next chapter.

57 a-f. Six designs from *The Gardeners Labyrinth*. All are drawn with double lines to show how the design is woven together, but no shading has been used so the two-dimensional appearance suggests patterns taken from flat decorative designs.

58 *above*. The knot design from *The Gardeners Labyrinth* which is very similar to one of the knots in Hovenden's map of All Souls, Oxford (plate 53).

From the point of view of knots the most intriguing publication to appear in England in the second half of the sixteenth century was *A Short Instruction Verie Profitable and Necessarie for All Those that Delight in Gardening,* translated out of French as the title-page tells us, and published in London in 1591. This is a very rare book of just 24 pages and the British Library has only the 1592 edition, but it contains some original woodcuts of knots not found in any other publication (plates 61 and 64).

How different is the design in plate 61 to anything else considered so far. It appears to be two squares of ribbon-like edged material, woven together, with four identical leafy ornaments straddling the corners like swags and the Tudor rose at the centre; it is reminiscent of the embroidered designs of Claude Mollet's parterres to be discussed later. The publication contains many illustrations which appeared in Thomas Hill – the woodcuts of how to water the garden, the arbour, and the embroiderer's 'propre knot' from the *Proffitable Arte* (1568) (plate 51) and the maze designs – showing again how usual it was to pass woodblocks from one printer to another. However there is also a group of delightful and unique examples (plate 64) – four knots drawn, without any shading, in the quarters of a garden, surrounded by stylised trees in profile. These designs are all very

threadlike and surely taken from embroiderers' pattern-books; they are very similar to some that were copied into Thomas Trevelyon's 'Miscellany for all Craftsmen'.

*The Orchard, and the Garden* appeared anonymously in 1594 (a translation 'Gathered from the Dutch and French') with numerous designs for knots, all of which can be traced to the 1586 edition of *Maison Rustique* (plates 63 a-c). They have shading in the figures alluding to their three-dimensional construction and making them in some ways less applicable to embroidery. They are based on the square, and with their intricate weaving patterns can better be compared with the Celtic knotwork in chapter one and the emerging styles of Flemish strapwork than with the designs in Thomas Hill. Other publications were to take up these designs, and indeed, *The Country-mans Recreation* bound with *The Expert Gardener* (a reprint of *The Orchard and the Garden* with a new title) in 1640, indicate that even by the middle of the seventeenth century knot designs were still continuing to be planted as they had been over the last fifty years.

*L'Agriculture et Maison Rustique* (1570) has already been mentioned. It was first written and published in Latin in 1554 by the physician Charles Estienne under the title *Praedium Rusticum* and began to exert an influence on English garden designs in the last quarter of the sixteenth century. Unlike the publications of Thomas Hill or any of the other English garden books that have been referred to where practically no information was given about the planting of knots, Charles Estienne included some historical and practical information describing how knots were to be planned and constructed. It was left to Jean Liébault, another physician, to bring out an augmented and revised edition in 1586 with numerous illustrations of parterre designs. According to Liébault these are the work of 'M.Porcher, prior of Crecy-en-Brie, the most excellent in this art not only in France but in all Europe'. (It was one of these designs which had appeared in *The Gardeners Labyrinth*, 1594, plate 56). This information became more readily available in England after Richard Surflet brought out a translation of *Maison Rustique* in 1600 using the title *Maison Rustique, or The Countrie Farme.*

In the first French edition of 1570 there is a clear definition of the parterre, and Surflet translates it simply as the 'flower garden'. However the word provokes confusion because Surflet uses 'knot' to describe the designs which are called parterres in the French edition of 1586. *Entrelacs* (interwoven work) is the French equivalent for the knot motif but this word is not used in *Maison Rustique* to describe the knotted designs. Further it is sometimes thought that 'parterre' derives from 'partiri' to divide (see Derek Clifford's *History of Garden Design*), whereas Clifford correctly points out parterre comes from '*par terre*' meaning 'on the ground'. However the French flower garden or parterre was indeed

divided into compartments – each compartment was based on the square and there were different kinds. '*Un compartiment simple*' was a single square of one continuous design, and certainly knots (*entrelacs*) were a feature or features of these compartments. Where a compartment was made up of several sections with different designs it was described as a '*parterre de carreaux rompus*', which can be translated as a parterre of separate designs without knots (*carreau* is literally a tile or small square and *rompu* means broken). If some of the separate designs were made up of knots, the parterre

**59. The knot garden in front of the old manor house at Hatfield.**

**60. The 'Rainbow' portrait of Queen Elizabeth I (Hatfield House, *c*.1600-03) with the coiled serpent on her sleeve, here interpreted as a symbol of wisdom. Her dress is richly embroidered with pinks, heart's ease, honeysuckle and other flowers much favoured in Tudor gardens.**

NON SINE SOLE
IRIS.

would be described as a 'parterre de carreaux rompus, avec compartiments simples'. The 'propre knot' (plate 56) in the later edition of Thomas Hill's *Gardeners Labyrinth* (1594) is described in *Maison Rustique* as having a 'bordure avec son compartiment simple'; in English it would be said the design had a border of knots with a single knot design in the centre.

Just as Hill advised the planting of thyme and hyssop to make the knots, so *Maison Rustique* included instructions for what to use for the compartments but provided rather more choice than Hill: pennyroyal, hyssop, wild thyme, rosemary, thyme, sage, marjoram and chamomile are all recommended, but note the exclusion of box which comes in for strong criticism:

as for boxe in as much as it is of a naughtie smell, it is to be left of and not dealt withall... It must not be planted neere the place where bees are kept, for the flower killeth them

soddainly. Some affirme that it corrupteth the aire by the stinking smell it hath, and for this cause it would be as sparingly planted in the garden as possiblie may be. (from Surflet 1600)

The conclusion from this and other sources must be that the advice against the use of box was followed in England to the end of the century, and that box had no place in the sixteenth-century English knot garden.

In France, though, Claude Mollet, writing about his gardening experience, says he was the first to use box for parterres at St-Germain in 1595. It will be evident in the next chapter that the prejudice against box began to subside in England in the first decade of the seventeenth century – no doubt influenced by views from across the channel.

In the early years of the Stuart succession, Gervase Markham and William Lawson were the key figures. They continued the direction of knot-making as laid down by Hill and set out in *Maison Rustique*. It is important to keep in mind that both Markham and Lawson had come from a background of practical knowledge about gardens and country matters, whereas Hill apparently had no such knowledge. Markham, born about 1568, was known as a famous breeder of horses, and in his later years turned to writing from the stand-point of a comfortably off family of worthy landowners. In 1613 he brought out *The English Husbandman* which was the perfect English equivalent to the *Maison Rustique*, on which he relied heavily. He gives a full account of 'a garden of pleasure', and exhorts the gardener to have 'diligence, industry and art'. The book is, after Surflet's translation of the *Maison Rustique*, the most explicit in providing a comprehensive approach to the pleasure garden, with very detailed information on the laying

**61** *far left*. **This design from** *A Short Instruction Verie Profitable and Necessarie for All Those that Delight in Gardening* **(1591) with the Tudor rose at the centre is so different from anything published by Thomas Hill and looks more like the** *embroiderie* **that appears later with the work of André Mollet (plate 82).**

**63 a-c** *near right*. **Three knot designs from** *Maison Rustique* **(1586). They were later published in London in an English translation by Richard Surflet with the title** *Maison Rustique, or the Countrie Farm* **(1600). After that they reappeared in Markham's edition of** *The Countrey Farm* **(1616) and other works.**

**62** *left*. **Gervase Markham published this garden plan in** *The English Husbandman* **(1613). It shows a garden divided into four quarters and gives a good idea how the quarters could be used to include knots, emblems and heraldry. It is reminiscent of the garden of New College, Oxford, as seen in Loggan's engraving (plate 81)**

64 *right*. A remarkable illustration from *A Short Instruction* (1591) with trees in profile surrounding the plan of a garden with unusual knots in the four quarters.

out of paths, hedges and knots. He continues to adopt the square for knots, and advises very precisely on the laying out of alleys between them: they should be seven or eight feet wide and covered with sand and small gravel, powder of marble, or paving – the same instruction as appeared in the 1586 edition of *Maison Rustique*.

On the outside around the quarters of the garden he recommends a hedge of 'Primpe [privet], Boxe, Lavandar, Rose-mary, or such like', and for this he says 'Boxe is the best'. Here then, at the beginning of the seventeenth century, is a changed attitude to box. No longer is the smell unpleasant and even harmful, but instead box is now good on account of its lasting qualities. But when it comes to setting out the knots in the quarters Markham appears to rely on the earlier advice of Hill, though with a longer list of suitable plants: 'set it either with Germander, Issoppe, Time, or Pinke gilly-flowers', but, he says, 'Germander is the most principall best for this purpose'. For the drawing of the colours of arms and ensigns he is specific: yellow = clay, white = chalk, green = chamomile. Here there is no undue concern for how the colours are created – plants or other materials are equally suitable. Most of the figures which appear here have already appeared in *Maison Rustique* (plates 63 a-c).

It is thought that William Lawson, a Yorkshireman,

was a friend of Gervase Markham, as their publications frequently appeared together. In Lawson's *A New Orchard and Garden* (1618) there is for the first time a plan of a small country house garden showing how the ground was divided into quarters, with a graphic image for the function of each square in the garden (plate 70). The knot garden is clearly shown opposite the orchard, a round design within a square, and then two interlacing triangles with the Tudor rose at the centre. In Lawson's book, *The Countrie Housewifes Garden* (1617), the title-page makes a point of announcing that it is published 'together with divers new knots for gardens', and indeed these are an original set of knots that do not appear to have been published in any of the earlier garden books (plates 68 and 71). They are all drawn with shading to suggest their solid three-dimensional quality; they are all named, and ones like 'The Frette' and 'Lozenges' look as though they are adapted from carpenters' or glaziers' pattern books (see Gedde *Booke of Sundry Draughtes*, plate 18), or inspired by Gothic tracery (plate 15). Lawson gives no overbearing instructions on the laying out of the knots, for he says: 'they are as many, as there are devices in gardiners braines....The number of formes, mazes and knots is so great, and men are so diversely delighted, that I leave every House wife to herself... let her view these few, choice, new forms, and note this generally, that all plots are square, and all are bordered about with Privit, Rasens, Fleaberries, Roses, thorne, Rosemaris, Bee-flowers, Isop, Sage, or such like'.

Lawson continues to treat mazes alongside knots, and, not surprisingly, the maze included here is the same one as was printed in *The Gardeners Labyrinth* (1577). In contrast to Markham box is not mentioned as a plant to surround the quarters, or indeed to make the knots.

In spite of the obvious appreciation of knot gardens in Lawson and the fact that Markham calls attention to the 'beautifying of gardens' with 'mens braines hourely begetting and bringing forth such new garments and imbroidery for the earth', there is an inkling of changing fashions in Markham when he writes that knot gardens, although much admired in the past, are becoming unpopular among the wealthy, and are being replaced, as he says, by 'novelties': 'To beginne therefore with that which is most ancient and at this day of most use amongst the vulgar though least respected with great ones, who for the most part are wholy given over to novelties: you shall understand that Knots and Mazes were the first that were received into admiration'. It is not clear what he means by 'novelties', but it can be assumed that 'fashion' was continuing to spread from France where the emphasis was moving towards simple compartments, that is, in the English sense, without knots but with more 'embroidery', and that sweet smelling herbs were being supplanted (literally) by the widespread use of box. Further, that the knot garden as a cherished (and symbolic) square was being replaced by panels of different sizes, a variety of shapes, and an overall increase in size.

There are other sources too which could suggest that knots were increasingly thought of with disdain. Shakespeare in *Love's Labour's Lost* speaks of 'thy curious-knotted garden', and Francis Bacon in his famous essay *Of Gardens* (1597, but not published until 1625) dismisses practices associated with the knot garden: 'As for the making of knots or figures, with divers coloured earths, that they may be under the windows of the house, or that side which the garden stands, they be but toys; you may see as good sights many times in tarts'. But he does recommend the 'ordering of the ground...not too busy or full of work', which suggests that knots were too intricate for him, and instead he wants simply 'little low hedges, round like welts, with some pretty pyramids'. This could mean that Bacon was aware of the 'new' parterre, and the 'pretty pyramids' – styles and fashions which were spreading from France.

In this chapter knot gardens have been considered almost entirely through those books which illuminate the subject and little mention has been made of the gardens themselves. The reasons for this will be clear from the two following cases. One of the great houses belonging to William Cecil, Lord Burghley, was Theobalds where Queen Elizabeth was entertained in splendour on twelve occasions. It had one of the outstanding gardens of Elizabethan England, but virtually nothing on the ground, either of house or garden, remains to testify to its magnificence. Almost all that is known about the manor and its surroundings has been deduced from the

65, 66 and 67. At Morville Dower House in Shropshire, Katherine Swift, after much research in early garden books, has planned a small knot garden based on the work of Thomas Hill, *Maison Rustique* and a design taken from the carved oak panelling at a local Elizabethan house, Benthall Hall, near Much Wenlock (*left*). She has concentrated on those herbs referred to by Thomas Hill and others – lavender, germander and rue to mark the main lines of the design – avoiding the use of box. The beds are edged with upright planks with turned finials at the corners, in the manner of the woodcuts included in Thomas Hill's *Gardeners Labyrinth* (plate 69).

words of contemporary travellers like Paul Hentzner, but for detailed information on the layout of the 'great garden' to the south of the house, no better account survives than the Parliamentary Survey carried out in 1650. However in this excerpt, although it is evidently about the survival of an overall scheme from the middle years of Queen Elizabeth's reign, the planting and use of box reflects a garden of the seventeenth century:

One garden called the Greate Garden, adioyninge North on the afforesaid Cloyster lyinge under the Kinges Presence Chambers, and others, incompassed East, South, and West with a good brick wall, and North with the Capitall house...in the said Garden there are nine large compleate squares or knotts lyinge upon a Levell in the middle of the said Garden, whereof one is sett forth with box borders in the likenesse of the Kinges armes, verrie artificiallie and exquisitely made; one other plott is planted with choice flowers; the other 7 knotts are all grasse knotts, handsomely turfed in the intervalls or little walkes. All the afforesaid knotts are compassed aboute with a Quicksett hedge of White thorne, and privett, cutt into a handsome fashion; and at everie angle or corner standes a faire cherrie tree of a greate groth, with a Ciprus in the middle of most of the knotts, and at some of the corners...

The other case is Thomas Cecil's house at Wimbledon (begun in 1588), of which nothing remains today but a detailed plan of 1609 by the Elizabethan architect, Robert Smythson. Together with a Parliamentary Survey carried out in 1649, this provides a comprehensive view at that time of the survival of the Elizabethan garden with extensive seventeenth-century additions. The meticulous survey once again indicates the presence of the earlier garden overtaken by later styles and developments:

...the said Uper or Great Garden is divided into two several levels or parts... The said Lower Level is divided and cut out into 4 great squares, the two middlemost whereof contain within them eight several squares, and well ordered knotts, stored with the roots of very many and choice flowers; bordered with box, well planted and ordered, in the points, angles, squares, and roundlets; the four innermost quarters thereof being paved with Flanders bricks in the intervals, spaces, or little walks thereof;... The said eight knotts are

compassed about on three sides thereof with very handsome rails, piked with spired posts in every corner and angle, all of wood, varnished with white, [which] very much adorns and sets forth the Garden; all along the insides of which rails grow divers Cypress trees in a very decent order, having the outsides bordered with choice and pleasant flowers. (these two quotations are from the transcription in Amherst's *History of Gardening in England*)

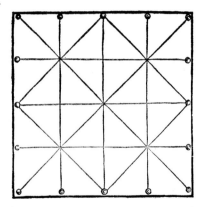

It surely comes as some surprise to find descriptions of white painted rails and pointed posts at every corner of the knots, when these are so closely associated with the Tudor garden. It is a reminder that fashions are sometimes slow to change, and from this account there is not a hint that the word 'parterre' had yet come into general use in place of the word 'knot'.

68 *left*. Two illustrations from *The Countrie Housewifes Garden*. The top one is called 'The ground plot for knots' and is clearly showing how a grid of lines is laid out on the ground as a preliminary to tracing out the knots. The method is the same as that drawn out and recommended in *Maison Rustique* (1586).

69 *opposite below*. This illustration appeared in many of Thomas Hill's books and shows an Elizabethan gardener planting up raised beds constructed with boards and turned finials at the corners. This idea was used by Katherine Swift for her garden at Morville (plates 65 and 67).

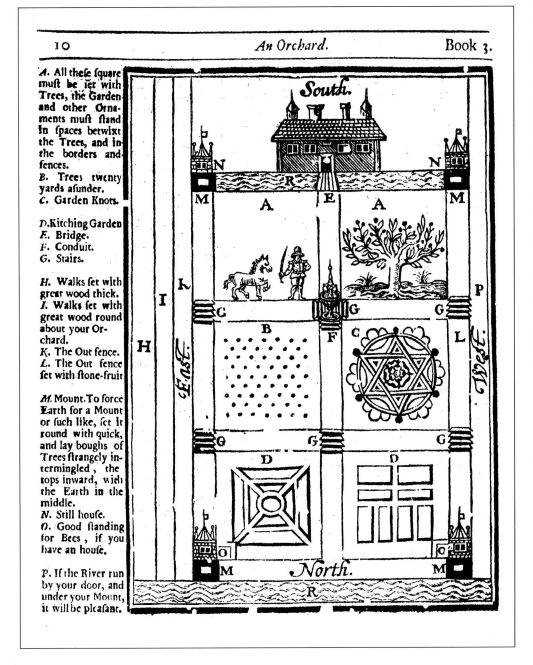

71 *above*. William Lawson's *The Countrie Housewifes Garden* (1617) included a number of very solid looking designs as if from pattern books for a three-dimensional craft. 'The Frette' and 'Lozenges' shown here suggest woodwork screens. William Lawson comments on the designs that 'they are as many, as there are devices in gardiners braines'.

70 *left*. This plan of a small country house garden from William Lawson's *A New Orchard and Garden* (1618) is one of the earliest to be published in a garden book. The knot garden at C is similar to some of those appearing in Thomas Hill's books.

# CHAPTER FOUR

# FROM KNOTS TO PARTERRES
## 1625-1714

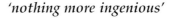

*'nothing more ingenious'*

Garden artifice reached its apogee of elaboration and sophistication during the seventeenth century, particularly in France where gardens such as the Tuileries in Paris displayed marvels of plant 'embroidery', and where later in the century the landscape of Versailles was developed on an hitherto unimaginable scale. The influence of such work spread to Britain with the great parterres at Wilton in the early part of the century, and then, towards the end, with the expansion of the formal gardens at Hampton Court and the *patte d'oie,* or goosefoot of avenues, across the park (plates 74 and 98).

Numerous gardening books were published in the seventeenth century, many with intricate engravings for knot gardens and parterres, as well as plans for entire garden layouts. Paintings of gardens were produced almost like family portraits, particularly the so-called 'bird's-eye view' perspectives, such as those by Kip and Knyff at the turn of the century, which provide startlingly accurate documentary views of many of the most important country houses of the day. Botanical exploration of the world was advancing rapidly and increasing numbers of plants were being sent back from abroad, greatly augmenting the opportunities for planting out knots and parterres with ever larger and more colourful ranges of flowers.

In Britain the introduction of Renaissance ideas in the early seventeenth century was dominated by the architect Inigo Jones (1573-1652), who had spent several years in Italy between about 1593 and 1603, and again from 1612 to 1614. He returned to establish the concept of planning houses and gardens together as a unity, and although, with the exception of Arundel House, it is difficult to attribute any specific garden designs to him, his influence dominated many aspects of the visual arts until the outbreak of the Civil War.

Just as Elizabethan styles of architecture gave way

to Jacobean and the increasing use of classical features and the dominance of planned design, so knot gardens were to be overtaken by the parterre. In the previous chapter the use of the word parterre in the *Maison Rustique* was seen to be an exact equivalent to the knot garden in England. Gradually the distinction between the two became more apparent as the seventeenth century progressed, and the knot garden quietly passed out of fashion, being seen as belonging to the bygone Elizabethan age. In place of 'knots' gardening books took up the word 'parterre', with a particular meaning in English best describing those French designs which exhibited a wealth of detailed embroidered shapes. In spite of this infiltration of the word parterre, the use of the term knot garden did not disappear from garden writing until the end of the century.

*Le Thrésor des Parterres de l'Univers* by D. Loris was published in Geneva in 1629, with the text in French, German and English giving detailed instructions on how to lay out gardens in squares with compartments and alleys. Although this is a comparatively rare book, the acceptance of the parterre across the Continent seems to be implied by its publication in several languages. In England in the same year John Parkinson published what Eleanour Sinclair Rohde called 'that most lovable of all gardening books', the *Paradisi in Sole Paradisus Terrestris,* whose title means 'the terrestrial paradise of the park in the sun' and is thus a clever pun on the author's name. This book is a milestone in gardening literature, and is the first to deal with flowers and the flower garden as an aspect of floriculture, rather than the 'herbals' which had been published hitherto, such as Gerard's in 1597, which emphasised the uses of plants rather than the pleasure to be derived from their flowers. Parkinson himself said he had seen many herbals, but no books devoted exclusively to the description of plants suitable for 'my Garden of pleasant and delightfull Flowers' (from 'The Epistle to the Reader' printed at the beginning), and significantly he calls the second chapter 'The frame or forme of a Garden of delight and pleasure, with the generall varieties thereof'. Concerning 'form' he can be seen as still adhering to the old schemes, for he dismisses the round garden and says the 'foure square forme' is the most usually acceptable to all. He includes six designs for 'knots'

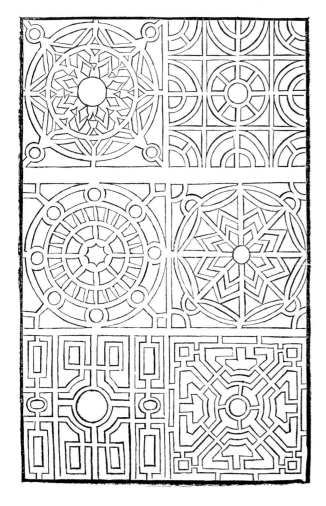

(plate 73), all basically geometric patterns with no knots as such, and provides details of how they should be arranged: 'To forme it therfore with walks, crosse the middle both waies, and round about it also with hedges, with squares, knots and trayles, or any other worke within the foure square parts, is according as every

74. Wilton House, Wiltshire. Isaac de Caus, the hydraulic engineer, produced a valuable record of his designs, published about 1645. This illustration shows the complete layout below the south front with the latest fashion for the French style of *parterre de broderie* in the foreground.

mans conceit alloweth of it'. Although Parkinson suggests that 'every man...take what may please his mind', he goes on to give a good reason why he has included models: 'And because many are desirous to see the formes of trayles, knots, and other compartments, and because the open knots are more proper for these Outlandish flowers; I have here caused some to be drawne, to satisfie their desires'. Parkinson does not make it clear what he is describing by using the word 'trayles'; it is likely that he is referring to the 'trailing' hedges which make up the design, but alternatively 'trail' can refer to a trellis for training climbing plants. Simple unlaced 'open knots' are now preferred for growing flowers – those 'outlandish' flowers recently introduced – so the emphasis has moved away from virtuoso knot designs. However, he still gives precise instructions as to the kinds of material that should be used for the patterns:

It is necessary also, that I shew you the severall materials, wherewith these knots and trayles are set forth and bordered; which are of two sorts: The one are living herbes, and the other are dead materials; as leade, boords, bones, tyles,

73 *left*. John Parkinson's *Paradisi in Sole* (1629) includes these six geometric knot designs which form simple compartments lacking the entwined knots that were characteristic of the Elizabethan period. Parkinson's knots were examples for gardeners to use, but he adds, 'every man ... take what may please his mind'.

72 *previous page*. The Privy Garden, Hampton Court Palace, London. William and Mary's Privy Garden has been magnificently restored after the most careful archaeological and archival research.

76 *right*. Wilton House, Wiltshire. A detail of the *parterre de broderie* which can be seen in the general layout in the foreground to either side of the main parterre (plate 74). The design is also reproduced again much later in Blake's *The Compleat Gardeners Practice* (1664).

75. This is a detail of an engraving made of the 1623 ceiling of the state bedroom at Boston House, Brentford. The series of geometric compartments bear comparison with Parkinson's designs and can also be usefully compared with the parterre designs for Wilton House (plate 76).

etc. [And for plants] ...Thrift. This is an everliving greene herbe, which many take to border their beds, and set their knots and trayles, and therein much delight, because it will grow thicke and bushie, and may be kept, being cut with a paire of Garden sheeres.

He is however also critical of the use of thrift because he comments that it can outgrow the knot or trayle and also die with the frost. He mentions germander, hyssop, marjoram, savory and thyme as often used; a list that is quite familiar since the Elizabethan period. But he goes further, and says that of all those mentioned he does not particularly recommend any, but he does favour box above all, 'Which lastly, I chiefly and above all other herbes commend unto you'. At last then, here is general approval in England that box is the best plant for all knot and parterre designs.

John Tradescant (died 1638), gardener and plant collector (particularly for Robert Cecil at Hatfield), was a friend of Parkinson and in 1626 went to live in Lambeth, where his garden became famous. Tradescant is buried in the churchyard of St Mary's and in 1976 the church was taken over as the Museum of Garden History. Next to Tradescant's tomb is the seventeenth-century garden designed by Lady Salisbury (plate 125).

One of the exceptional garden layouts in this period was created at Wilton in the 1630s for the 4th Earl of Pembroke by the famous hydraulic engineer, Isaac de Caus. Very little now remains of the formal gardens, but the documentation we have in the form of engraved designs is a unique record and was published in *Le Jardin de Wilton*, about 1645. The estate accounts for Wilton record that between 1632 and 1635 considerable sums were spent on completing the gardens which were laid out in front of the newly designed south front, which is generally attributed to Inigo Jones. The entire layout can be seen in the accompanying illustration (plate 74), with the garden broadly divided into three areas: the parterre in the foreground which would have been seen from the *piano nobile* of the house, then behind that the wilderness area concealing the natural diagonal course of the River Nadder, and then beyond an oval garden of alleys, walks and arbours, all surrounding a statue of a gladiator. The southern boundary of the garden was formed

by a raised balustraded terrace from which visitors could look down on the garden. The elaborate garden of four *parterres de broderie* was laid out in quarters around four fountains, each with a classical renaissance statue at the centre. The style of the *broderie* reflects some of the work of the Frenchman Claude Mollet, with a pattern, probably of box, looking like Jacobean strapwork dividing the embroidered compartments. At each side there are four additional parterres with similar structures and

small fountains at their centres. Wilton no doubt was at the height of fashion with garden parterres designed in the latest French manner, but as there are no other such detailed records of gardens at this time, it is difficult even to speculate how widespread such examples were. All the published documentation suggests that Wilton was unusual and that Elizabethan-style knots went on being grown in most gardens at this time with only a minority adopting the new style from across the water.

After Parkinson no other significant gardening books were published up to the establishment of the Commonwealth in 1649, with the exception of *The Expert Gardener* (1640), which has already been referred to in the previous chapter and where the designs were reprinted from *The Orchard and the Garden* (1594). This indicates that the old designs were still being used and further evidence comes from the more traditional kinds of designs found on the garden plans of Walter Stonehouse, Rector of Darfield, Yorkshire, who planted the garden there on his arrival in 1631. In the model, as he calls it, dated 1640, all the designs are based on the square (the bottom two are rectangles which are matched with the two above which are square); each one is a different design although all four of them are arranged as quarters around a central ornamental feature (plate 79). An article on his garden in the *Gardeners' Chronicle* (May 1920) describes the arrangement:

The beds in the style of the sixteenth century may have been the work of an earlier incumbent. They were laid out in five 'knots', perhaps enclosed with tile, stone or Box edgings, which bordered the 'forthrights', as the broader walks were called. According to the plan the beds in the knots were two and three feet in width, and would as Parkinson (1629) recommended, have contained the greater part of the herbaceous collection.

From the scale rule the main knots can be calculated to be twenty-seven paces square, and each compartment is given a number. Walter Stonehouse was known as a scholar with a keen interest in botany and he grew many rare and recently introduced plants; he left a complete list of plants with numbers corresponding to the compartments.

The 'fifth' knot at the top of the plan, the one squeezed into the irregular shape of the garden, has been used as the basis for a recreated knot garden at Moseley Old Hall in Staffordshire (plate 78). For ease of maintenance different coloured local shingles have been used in the box edged compartments instead of the flowers which are listed on the plan.

In France Claude Mollet had been active as the gardener to Henry IV from the late sixteenth century onwards and, as well as designing the gardens at St-Germain, already mentioned as the place where he introduced box into the parterre, he was responsible for the new gardens in the Tuileries to the west of the Louvre. At this time Mollet's parterre designs were first illustrated in Olivier de Serres's *Théâtre d'Agriculture* (1600), and resembled those published later in Jacques Boyceau's *Traité du Jardinage* (1638); many of the designs

were published in Mollet's posthumous work *Théâtre des Plans et Jardinages* (1652). The other important work on the French parterre at this time was *Le Jardin de Plaisir* (1651) by Claude Mollet's son André. Given that both these books were published during the interregnum in Britain, it is not surprising that their impact in England was not felt until after the Restoration (1660). The English edition, *The Garden of Pleasure,* did not appear until 1670.

In Britain one of the most revealing sources on gardening during the Commonwealth was written by Thomas Hanmer (1612-78), reflecting on his garden at his home at Bettisfield, Wrexham, in North Wales. His writings dating from 1659 existed only in manuscript until they were published with an introduction by Eleanour Sinclair Rohde in 1933. Where he refers to the knot garden it is worth quoting his text at some length:

...the whole designs or laying out of garden grounds are much different from what our fathers used, but the inward part of works also. In these days the borders are not hedged

This Figure represents Lines how they ought to be layde before you begin to drawe a large Knott but especially that following, And allso note that these Lines are not to be stirred till the Knott be finisht, and so by the use of these Lines and two lines more you may draw any Knott. This figure is supposed to contayne. 18: yards square & allowing. 21: Inches to each footpath.

77 and 78. Stephen Blake published this diagram in *The Compleat Gardeners Practice* (1664). It shows how to lay out a knot garden and is evidently very similar to the design at Moseley Old Hall, Staffordshire shown opposite. The recreated knot at Moseley Old Hall was in fact taken directly from the plans of Walter Stonehouse for his garden (plate 79).

about with privet, rosemary or other such herbs which hide the view and prospect, and nourish hurtful worms and insects, nor are standard fruit trees suffered to grow so high or thick as to shadow and cumber the soyle, but all is now commonly near the house laid open and exposed to the sight of the rooms and chambers, and the knots and borders are upheld only with very low coloured boards or stone, or tile. If the ground be spacious, the next adjacent quarters or *parterres,* as the French call them, are often of fine turf, but as low as any green to bowl on; cut out curiously into embroidery of flowers and shapes of arabesques, animals or birds, or *feuillages,* and the small alleys or intervals filled with several coloured sands and dust with much art, with but few flowers in such knots, and those only such as grow very low, least they spoil the beauty of the embroidery.

Those remote from habitation are compartments, as they call them, which are knots also, and borders destined for flowers, yet sometimes intermixed with grasswork, and on the outside beautified with vases on pedestals, or dwarf cypresses, firs, and other greens which will endure our

79 *bottom left.* **Walter Stonehouse's 'model', as he calls it, for his garden at Darfield, Yorkshire (1640). The top right hand knot design has been used for the garden at Moseley Old Hall shown on the previous page.**

80 *left.* **The re-drawn 'Proper' knot as published in the new edition of** *The Gardeners Labyrinth* **(1652). It is now very different from its first appearance in 1568 (see plate 51) and reflects the changes in fashion which had taken place by the middle of the seventeenth century.**

81 *right, above.* **New College, Oxford. David Loggan's engraving of 1675 shows a spectacular mount above a parterre laid out in four quarters which include a living sundial and the king's arms.**

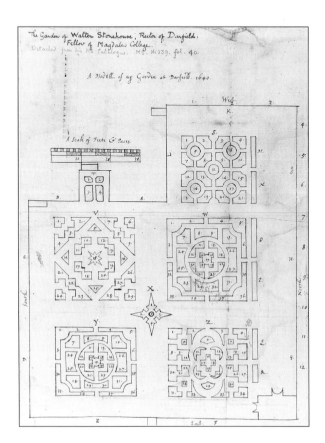

winters, set uniformly, at reasonable distances from each other, and in these great grounds beyond are either labyrinths with hedges cut to a man's height, or thickets for birds cut through with gravely walks, or you have variety of alleys set with elms, limes, abeles, firs and pines, with fountains, cascades and statues.

His first point is that the laying out of gardens had much changed since the late Elizabethan period, but it is not entirely clear what kind of changes he is referring to. His reference to the gardens being 'near the house laid open and exposed' suggests a more formal or planned relationship between house and garden, and the garden being less enclosed with walls, galleries and courtyards also indicates that gardens are beginning to extend outwards into the landscape, rather as in the French manner. Undoubtedly the knots or parterres – apparently the words for him are interchangeable in that they refer to a form of design – have changed dramatically from the stiff geometric knots of his father's generation to new configurations of embroidery, arabesques and *feuillages* (foliage), making up the design of the knot. He also stresses the importance of low growing flowers and herbs 'least they spoil the beauty of the embroidery'. Rohde in her introduction observes that at the time Hanmer was writing the flowers which would have em-

82 *right.* **Claude Mollet's designs for the** *parterre de broderie* **were published in** *Le Jardin de Plaisir* **(1651). This example is indicative of the French influence that will be seen in England towards the end of the seventeenth century.**

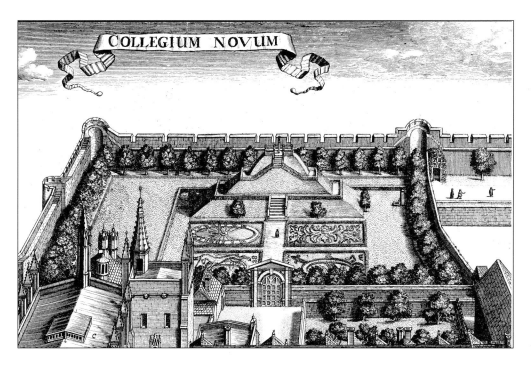

bellished the knot had only been introduced during the last fifty years – tulips, the crown imperial, Tradescant's great double narcissus, martagon lilies, the yellow crocus, double hepaticas, lychnis, *Lobelia cardinalis*, nasturtiums, and others. It should be noted too that in his wider description of the parterre, with vases and clipped evergreens, Hanmer is describing the kind of garden that is more typical of the period after the Restoration, but labyrinths are still firmly part of the garden's design, although now no longer in the form of a low-growing shrub (or foot) maze but rather the tall hedge type which became popular in the seventeenth century.

It is curious to note that at much the same time as Hanmer was writing his work on gardens, *The Gardeners Labyrinth* was reprinted (1652), with essentially the same text as the first publication of 1577, but now the 'Proper knots to be cast in the quarters of a Garden' (same title as used before) have been redrawn with the intention no doubt of making the book look more up to date (plate 80). The new designs, although lacking in detail, do not appear to reflect exotic French fashions; the shaded areas refer to shapes cut into turf, or alternatively the shapes could be outlined with box, although the drawing does not seem to suggest this.

One of the key events of the Commonwealth years was the unsuccessful attempt by Prince Charles to take the throne in 1651. After he lost the battle at Worcester, one of his hiding places was Boscobel House and its famous oak tree. This modest house therefore soon became a landmark, and not surprisingly drawings were made of the house and gardens at the time of the Restoration. The engraving by Hollar shows a formal knot garden of box compartments laid out in front of a small mount. Today the box gardens have been replanted in their original position below the mount which has survived although the timber shelter on top has replaced the original arbour where Prince Charles is supposed to have rested (plates 83-85). Mounts were a common feature of Tudor and Stuart gardens and their function was to give both a view of the country beyond and to provide an ideal view of the geometric knots in the garden. Another fine mount, this time stepped and terraced, can be seen in Loggan's engraving of New College (plate 81), with a 'parterre' laid out below it, showing quarters which include a living sundial and the King's arms – this arrangement should be compared with the very similar one in Markham's 'Plaine Square' (plate 62).

In her *British Botanical and Horticultural Literature before 1800* Blanche Henrey compared the number of books published on botany and horticulture in the sixteenth and seventeenth centuries and found that five times as many were published in the later period, and that of these the majority were published during the Commonwealth and after the Restoration. Surprisingly many of those published between 1660 and the end of the century continued to carry knot designs.

Stephen Blake's *The Compleat Gardeners Practice* (1664) gives very careful instructions on how to lay out a knot design (plate 77), not unlike the system printed some eighty years before in *Maison Rustique* from which many of his designs were copied. The compartmental design shown here, with instructions, is similar to the simple geometric form in the garden of Walter Stonehouse, while other designs show the French influence from earlier in the century including what amounts to a reproduction of one of the parterres printed in *Le Jardin de Wilton*. Blake (active 1660s) is known to have been a gardener to the gentry and so one assumes his book was based upon practice and was prepared as a guide to others – in this way he holds up yet another mirror to gardening activity in the early Restoration period. His writing has a simple and direct self-educated approach very different from the literary style of the day: 'But what remaineth at the present, but that you modelize and contrive your Garden-plots, by these few directions which I give you, or others, which you may better like of; and also to beautifie them with such knots as follow here-after of my invention, or those that may be invented by your selfe, which probably may please your fancy better than mine'.

There follows a 'True Lovers Knott' with a quaint verse underneath (plate 2), still very much in the Elizabethan tradition and again very similar in style to knot designs printed in the *Maison Rustique* of 1586 (plates 63b and c). Despite the inclusion of these 'traditional' style knots, overall the range shows examples of stylistic developments over the last half century including grass cut-work.

83, 84 and 85. Boscobel House, Shropshire, became a landmark after Prince Charles used it as a hiding place after the Battle of Worcester in 1651. This detail of an engraving by Wenceslaus Hollar (1660) shows the kind of garden which then surrounded the house. Today the garden has been recreated with box edged beds and the photograph opposite includes the mount which is also clearly visible in Hollar's engraving.

Shortly after *The Compleat Gardeners Practice* appeared another gardener, Leonard Meager, published *The English Gardener* in 1670. It includes a series of knot patterns prefaced with this introduction: 'And lastly, the ordering of the garden of pleasure, with diver's forms of knots, plat-forms, and wilderness work, etc.' He writes, 'Dutch or French Box, it is the handsomest, the most durable, and cheapest to keep', which underlines the significant place that box now held in the formation of knots and parterres, and he positively draws attention to the disadvantages of other plants saying that hyssop and thyme need cutting every few weeks, and germander does not keep well, although he says it was

'much used many years ago', and thrift is 'apt to gap'. In general his designs are made up of simple geometric shapes which look like cut outs, and could have been formed with turf or made into simple compartments which were then filled with flowers. One or two designs have embroidery embellishments in their quarters showing the direct influence of the *parterre de broderie*. The book was very popular and was enlarged and re-printed many times up to the early eighteenth century.

One of the designs from Meager was used in 1975 to recreate a knot garden at Little Moreton Hall (plate 86). Although the geometric forms are made up of simple shaded areas, without any indication of compartments, the interpretation of the design at Little Moreton was to outline the shapes with box and create 'open knots', which were filled with gravel rather than flowers.

Ham House in Richmond (see title-page and plate 144) is another example of careful 'restoration' (1975/76) of the splendid gardens that it was thought were laid out according to the plan by Slezer and Wyck, about 1671-72. Since then the more recent Helmingham plan of around 1730 has indicated that the earlier gardens never existed and instead it shows a much simpler lay-out of a grass lawn with a central statue. Undoubtedly the garden did have splendid parterres according to an account written by John Evelyn in 1678, but details of the precise nature of the design are lacking.

The decades from the Restoration through the reigns of William and Mary, and of Queen Anne, up to the beginning of the Hanoverian Succession, are dominated by two Continental influences – French and Dutch. Charles II who had spent much of his time in France during the interregnum became well aware of French taste, and this had been communicated to the visiting Scottish architect Sir William Bruce (1630-1710) who was responsible for laying out gardens in Scotland in the French manner. Bruce particularly admired the work of André Le Nôtre who had designed the magnificent gardens at Vaux-le-Vicomte between 1556 and 1661, and then created the immense royal gardens of Versailles for Louis XIV from 1665 onwards.

During 1688 Mary arrived in England from Holland, succeeding the ousted king, James II, to become queen with her Dutch husband, William. For the next fourteen years William replanned Hampton Court in the Dutch manner in the style of his royal palace at Het Loo, and set the fashion for what is known as the Anglo-Dutch garden. Between 1660 and 1714 – a period when royal gardens were made on an enormous scale – it is difficult to disentangle the strands of influence, particularly from France and Holland, that altered the style of British gardens, although general characteristics can be observed. For the knot-garden-cum-parterre, the balance slowly swung in the direction of the parterre with the term 'knot garden' almost abandoned by the end of the century. By the 1690s the formal garden, whether it can best be described as French or Dutch, exhibited parterres of increasing intricacy. Derek Clifford in his *History of Garden Design* noted: 'The *compartiment de broderie* was not the only kind of parterre. By the end of the seventeenth century the specialists had analysed their craft and described eleven different types'. Much earlier Inigo Triggs in *Formal Gardens* (1902) had concluded: 'This meretricious excess in the treatment of the parterre had much to do with the revulsion of taste which culminated in the introduction of the landscape garden'.

86, 87, and 88. Little Moreton Hall, Cheshire. The plan taken from Leonard Meager's book *The English Gardener* (1670) was used as the basis for this recreated garden of box compartments. By comparing the plan and the photographs of the garden it becomes clear that only the outlines of Meager's shapes have been used to make the compartments.

During this period of 'excess' two of the most widely known garden makers in England were George London (died 1714) and Henry Wise (1653-1738). Together they ran a business in planning new gardens and supplying plants to clients from their Brompton Park nurseries in London which were founded in 1681. Henry Wise, as well as being gardener to Queen Anne at Hampton Court, worked with George London in the making of what seems like countless prestigious gardens, many of them recorded in Kip and Knyff's engravings. Dyrham Park in Gloucestershire would be just one example (plate 91). Only a fragment of the so called Dutch garden can be seen over the roof of the house, but Stephen Switzer, who visited Dyrham in about 1708, left a vivid account of his walk round the garden and a neat description of the parterre: 'The Parterre is cut into four Quarters of Grass and Gravel, of various Forms, the Borders adjoining to the principal Gravel Walk, leading to the main Door of the Front, being set off with large Pyramid Silver Hollies, Ews, etc., having painted Iron Rods with gilded Nobs for their Support, and the Center-Sides, etc., with round-headed Laurels exactly clipt, Bays, small Pyrmid Ews, etc.'.

It would appear from the illustration that embroidered shapes or *feuillage* have been cut into the turf (*gazon coupé),* or outlined in dwarf box. This is a modest parterre, but a glance at *The Retir'd Gard'ner* (a translation of two books – Francois Gentil, 1704 and Louis Liger, 1706) published 'for our English Culture' by London and Wise in 1706, provides a full range of the most exuberant embroidered parterres. Liger writes, 'In my opinion there's nothing more ingenious belonging to a Garden, than the different Ways of marking out different Figures in a Parterre'. He goes on to define the different designs: 'Imbroidery is those Draughts which represent in Effect those we have on our Cloaths, and that look like Foliage, and these Sorts of Figures in Gard'ner's Language are call'd Branch-work. Below this Foliage certain Flowers seem to be drawn, which is that Part of Imbroidery which we call Flourishings'.

Louis Liger provides a full description of one of the parterres (plate 90):

The Imbroidery of this Parterre may be fill'd with what Earth we please, provided it be distinguish'd from that of the Cutwork, which gives to these sorts of Compartment the finest

**89** *above* **and 92** *below right.* **Tredegar House, Newport. An early archaeological study of the garden was carried out in the 1980s revealing the layout of a formal garden (about 1719-30) lying beneath later infill. This has been recreated, and is one of the few examples now to be seen of a parterre making extensive use of coloured materials.**

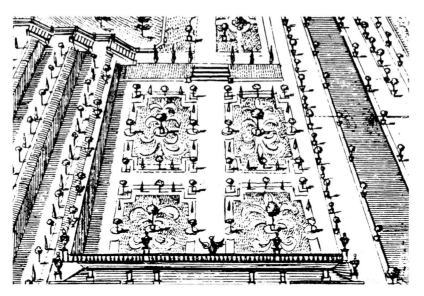

90 *far left*. This plate from London and Wise, *The Retir'd Gard'ner* (1706) is a good example of the French parterre which had now become fashionable in England. Useful comparison can be made between this, the plate from André Mollet (plate 82) and the one from John James (plate 93).

91 *left*. Dyrham Park, Gloucestershire. This detail from the bird's-eye view engraving by Kip (1712) graphically shows the garden as so accurately described by Stephen Switzer when he visited in about 1708.

Relievo that can be. The Paths of this Parterre must likewise be set off with yellow or white Gravel, and the Borders with an Earth like that of the Cut-work.

It should be evident from this that the fancy embroidery pieces are made with coloured materials; and elsewhere he mentions powdered tile, beaten charcoal and iron-filings and the 'yellowest sand', probably edged with box although he does not say so. In other examples the cut-work shape, which is outlined with edging stones or box to make the compartments, can be filled with flowers.

One other title is a marvellous source for details on

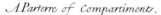
*A Parterre of Compartiments.*

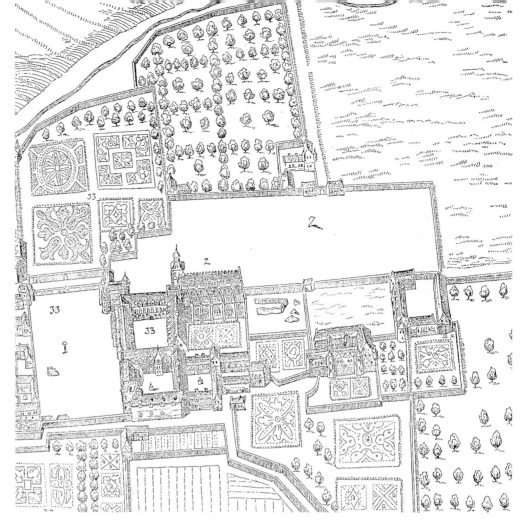

the parterre. John James's *The Theory and Practice of Gardening* (1712), which is a translation of the French original of Dezallier d'Argenville (1709), gives examples of gardens laid out on an enormous scale. It offers a definition of the word parterre, claiming that it comes from the Latin *partiri* meaning to divide, although the book allows that 'according to some, a Parterre denotes a flat and eaven Surface'. It gives all kinds of names for what it calls the 'branched and flourished work': palms, foliage, hawk-bills, sprigs, tendrils, volutes, knots, stalks, ties, husks, cartouches, plumes, frets or interlacing, shell-works, etc., and says there are 'divers Sorts of Parterres', but here reduces them to four: parterres of embroidery, compartment, parterres after the English manner, and cut-work.

The distinction he makes between the first two is that the embroidery parterre is symmetrical from side to side, and the compartment is symmetrical both 'in respect of the Ends, as of the Sides'. The English manner parterre he describes as 'the plainest and meanest of all' being made up of cut grass-work, *gazon coupé*, and

**93** *left.* 'A Parterre of Compartiments' from John James *The Theory and Practice of Gardening* (1712).

**94** *above.* An early plan of the Palace of Holyroodhouse in Edinburgh (1647) showing several intricate parterres laid out in the gardens surrounding the palace. It was examples like these which were used as a guide for the restoration of the gardens at Pitmedden in Grampian (plate 97).

**95 and 96** *right.* Two parterres from John James. The one described as in the English manner he calls 'the plainest and meanest of all', and for the other, a parterre of cutwork for flowers, he adds 'tho' not so fashionable at present, are however not unworthy our regard'.

A Parterre after ye English manner

fig. 1st

A Parterre of Cutwork for Flowers

**97. Pitmedden, Grampian. A view across the Great Garden showing the recreated parterres overlooked by the upper terrace.**

encompassed with a border of flowers. The cut-work parterre is defined as having neither embroidery nor grass-work, but only borders edged with box 'that serve to raise Flowers in', and by means of sanded paths 'you may walk through the whole Parterre'.

As virtually all knots and parterres disappeared under the relentless groundswell of changing opinion that personified 'Nature' as the ideal maker of the eighteenth-century landscape garden, there are now no surviving examples; however paintings, drawings and engravings of the seventeenth century depict extensive formal gardens surrounding country houses, just as they do around the chateaux of France. The parterre in differing degrees of elaboration played an essential part in the overall design.

It is possible to see parterres in Britain today as some examples have been authentically recreated. Mention has been made of Scottish gardens where the French influence was strong in the seventeenth century. It was particularly evident in the architecture and landscape design of Sir William Bruce, who had made

frequent visits to France during the Commonwealth years. From the symmetrical scheme and the axial plan for his own house at Kinross, it is clear that he designed the landscape with the work of Le Nôtre in mind.

One of Bruce's acquaintances was Sir Alexander Seton who inherited the family estates at Pitmedden. From the inscription on the doorway to the garden one learns that he 'founded' the garden on 2 May 1675. Unfortunately, although the essential structure of the garden – walls, terraces, steps and pavilions – have survived, all records of the parterres were lost. The National Trust for Scotland, who took over the property in 1951, decided to restore the garden and recreate the parterres. As a basis for the designs they chose the parterres which appear in an early engraving (1647) of the royal gardens of the Palace of Holyroodhouse which had been rebuilt by Sir William Bruce in 1671 (plates 94 and 97). At Pitmedden four great parterres were laid out on the southern terrace: one was created around a contemporary sundial with the legend 'Tempus Fugit' written out in box, another displays the coat-of-arms of Sir

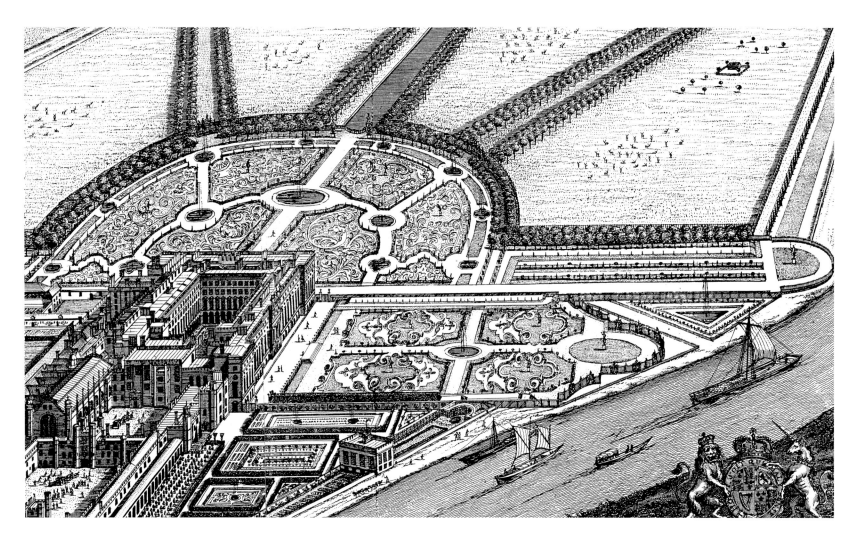

Alexander Seton and the date, and the remaining two are large extravaganzas of styles of *parterre de broderie*.

Another recreation has taken place more recently at Tredegar House (about 1664-72) in South Wales, where excavations in the walled gardens revealed the layout of an early formal garden (about 1719-30) lying beneath later infill. Two intricate parterres have now been restored with as much attention to the archaeological evidence as possible (plates 89 and 92).

In 1992 after much consultation it was agreed that the Privy Garden of William and Mary at Hampton Court should be restored. There was a great deal of documentary evidence on which to base the designs of the recreation, the most important of which were an early eighteenth-century plan of the parterre and the well known bird's-eye view painting of Hampton Court by Leonard Knyff (1702). Further evidence for the reconstruction was found during the course of excava-

tions when the trenches revealed the position and shape of the original fleur-de-lis patterns, and more information was gained from the discovery of the early drainage system and the plinths for the statuary.

The study and understanding of the knot and the parterre now regrettably enters a void, for the eighteenth century showed scant regard for the qualities of the formal garden after the rising tide of opinion led to the demise of what Inigo Triggs above scathingly called a 'meretricious excess'. This change in taste in the early years of the 1700s has been well documented in John Dixon Hunt and Peter Willis's *Genius of the Place* (1975). It is said that the 'scrollwork' parterre at Chatelherault in Scotland, originally made in 1730 and recently restored, is one of the last formal layouts in Britain before the landscape movement overshadowed the taste for formal gardening. We have to wait practically a century for its reappearance.

98. Bird's-eye view engraving of Hampton Court Palace and grounds by Johannes Kip after the painting by Leonard Knyff (1702). Such engravings are an invaluable record of the formal gardens of the period that were almost all obliterated by the English landscape garden of the eighteenth century.

99 *opposite*. The Privy Garden, Hampton Court Palace. This photograph was taken from the roof of the palace when a light covering of snow had brought out the pattern to perfection. During the archaeological excavations the fleur-de-lis outlines were precisely revealed.

100. Blenheim Palace, Oxfordshire. The water parterre designed by Achille Duchêne recalls the magnificent seventeenth-century one created at Versailles for Louis XIV.

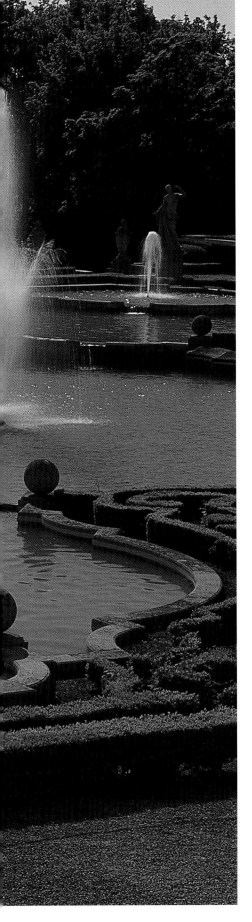

# CHAPTER FIVE

# REVIVALS AND RESTORATIONS
## AFTER 1800

*'That piece of hoarded loveliness'*

The search for architectural style was a leading preoccupation in the nineteenth century; in *The Gentleman's House* (1864) the architect Robert Kerr wrote about the architect's quandary over the need to find a style appropriate for the century. Such a dilemma had been far less apparent in the eighteenth century when what is now described as Georgian or Palladian became the accepted architectural style. After 1800, with the arrival of Neoclassicism, Charles Barry's Italianate villas, and the Gothic Revival, the nineteenth century seemed stylistically to have disintegrated into an eclecticism which could provide a style for all seasons – Jacobean, Gothic, Italian, Elizabethan, and so on. Landscape design was also dominated by revivals; in the middle of the century it was the Italianate garden, then the French or Dutch parterre – then after 1870 the Arts and Crafts movement introduced another revival, broadly medieval in spirit, and which in garden terms was a revival of the old English manor garden of the sixteenth and seventeenth century, such as that which was designed for Athelhampton in Dorset. This was to be the characteristic type in Blomfield's *Formal Garden in England* (1892).

At the start of the nineteenth century the written history of the garden had hardly been begun. George Johnson's *History of English Gardening* (1829) is one of the first attempts, but knots are hardly mentioned and Thomas Hill is rather disparagingly dismissed as a 'a hacknied compiler of books'. The most useful general outline history appeared in J.C.Loudon's *Encyclopaedia of Gardening* (1822), but, again with the exception of Hill, very little mention is made of the knot garden, although there are instructions for the laying out of embroidered seventeenth-century parterres. Confusion between knots and parterres, and French and Dutch garden styles, persisted in much of the literature of the time. M'Intosh in *The Flower Garden* (new edition 1839)

reprinted one of the knot designs from *Maison Rustique*. He captioned it 'Dutch Parterre' (plate 102), and wrote, 'The leading character of the Dutch style is rectangular formality, and what may sometimes be termed clumsy artifice, such as yew trees cut out in the intended form of statues'. He inveighed against such practices: 'The taste for these fancies still lingers among suburban amateur gardeners, notwithstanding the ridicule with which it has been so unsparingly treated by the press'. Any attempt to discover when the parterre reappeared as a garden feature will be inconclusive; some will even argue that parterre gardening of a kind was being practised throughout the eighteenth century in the flower garden and that its existence has, until recently, been overshadowed by the literary search for the 'natural landscape'.

One early and outstanding presentation of parterre designs, although not widely circulated, was the small book by C.F.Ferris called *The Parterre* (1837) which included seventeenth-century designs. However much more significant in the search for revivals of the parterre in the nineteenth century is the indefatigable and extremely influential John Claudius Loudon (1783-1843), who wrote much on gardens and provides the litmus test for changing fashions. In his *Suburban Gardener* (1838), there is an engraving of a 'French Parterre' in the garden of Mrs Lawrence's villa at Drayton Green in London (plate 104), and the same book includes a villa with a garden in what he calls the 'Geometrical Style' to demonstrate how 'the ancient style of laying out grounds can be adapted to modern uses'. In the plan of the garden the back of the house opens on to a raised terrace surrounding the flower garden which is described as an 'ancient parterre'. Loudon's other publications included the popular *Gardener's Magazine* (1826-44), which is an invaluable source on gardening matters of the time.

Given this background it is not surprising that in the

101. Drummond Castle, Perthshire. The extensive parterre, some 300 metres in length, survives today as one of the most spectacular in Scotland. It is one of the earliest revivals and was laid out in the form of a St Andrew's Cross by Lewis and George Kennedy in the 1820s and 1830s.

first half of the century there are many outstanding examples of patterned gardens which derive from the long history of the parterre. Drummond Castle in Scotland is a remarkable forerunner laid out in the form of a St Andrew's Cross by Lewis and George Kennedy in the 1820s and 1830s (plate 101). Also in Scotland at the same time plans were prepared for the restoration of a seventeenth-century garden at Drumlanrig Castle, but in the end none were carried out. Sir Charles Barry (1795-1860), architect of the Houses of Parliament, recreated an 'Elizabethan' garden at Gawthorpe Hall, Lancashire (about 1851), with a concentric scheme of geometric shaped beds, described sometimes as looking like a strapwork design, planted out with bedding, in front of the restored house of about 1600; this garden is now grassed over (plate 105). At Dunrobin, in Sutherland, Barry worked on the house and designed a magnificent parterre below the castle walls (plate 103).

At this time, to add confusion to the notion of the parterre, a revolutionary method of planting came into prominence. From the 1840s onwards, the so called 'bedding system' became *de rigueur* for all the great gardens of the mid century. Bedding out of half-hardy annuals, many of which had only been introduced into Britain in the nineteenth century, and their propagation in thousands was made possible by the vastly improved greenhouses of the day. The planting schemes, best viewed from above, were developed into all manner of shapes and were laid out in beds of ever increasing complexity, often referred to as parterres. If 'parterre' is taken literally as referring to the flower garden 'on the ground', and its design is loosely thought of as one of beds of different colours making up a pattern, then it is difficult to argue a case for not including a great many of the vast bedding schemes, such as at Trentham, Castle Ashby, and Longford Castle, as belonging

102 *below*. The so-called 'Dutch Parterre' from M'Intosh's *The Flower Garden* (1839) is copied from a design which appeared in *Maison Rustique* in 1586.

historically in the same category of gardening. (Marcus Binney's *Elysian Gardens* includes splendid photographs of many of these, see plate 109).

There was much discussion too as to the importance of the placing of colours so as to add to the quality of design. One who argued passionately on this subject was the Egyptologist, Sir Gardner Wilkinson. He instructed his readers that the garden near the house must be laid out in geometric patterns and demonstrated his laws of colour harmony in his book *On Colour and on the necessity for a general diffusion of taste among all classes*

103 *above left*. Dunrobin Castle, Sutherland. The Victorian architect Charles Barry was responsible for this great parterre of the 1840s below the castle walls.

105 and 106 *above*. Gawthorpe Hall, Lancashire. The marvellous Jacobean strapwork ceiling shown here could have inspired Charles Barry to plant the geometric parterre in the South Garden in about 1850. This is now grassed over.

104 *below left*. Mrs Lawrence's 'French Parterre' as it was published in *The Suburban Gardener*.

(1858). The illustration shown here is his example of how seven colours 'may be arranged in harmonious order' (plate 107); the Arabic looking design is not unlike some of our earlier geometric knot patterns (plate 73).

However, to avoid being deflected from the narrower definition of the parterre as practised in the seventeenth century, it is useful to consider the work

107 *far left*. **Sir Gardner Wilkinson published this geometric pattern in 1858 to demonstrate how seven colours may be arranged in harmonious order. These principles were to be applied to the making of geometric gardens and flower beds.**

of William Nesfield (1793-1881). He was certainly recognised in his time for a particular style of gardening associated with the French parterre and was an inspired exponent of this art. Indeed it is said that he travelled round visiting his clients carrying a portfolio of seventeenth-century engravings of parterres and would, as it were, wheel them out to demand, as examples of the kinds of design he was suggesting.

Nesfield's early career had apparently little to do with gardening: he was in the army for a short time before taking up painting which he practised solely and with some dedication for a number of years until he married in his late thirties and decided to make land-scape gardening his profession. Shortly after that he went to live at Fortis Green on Muswell Hill, where his brother-in-law, the architect Anthony Salvin, had built his house; Salvin was undoubtedly an important link in Nesfield's career for they had worked together for a number of years with Nesfield preparing garden plans for Salvin's houses. It was the opportune publication of the designs and description of his garden at Fortis Green in the *Gardener's Magazine* in 1840 that gave Nesfield wide publicity. In the article Loudon said, 'Mr. Nesfield has long been known as a landscape-painter...he has lately directed his attention to landscape gardening, and that with so much success that his opinion is now

108 *left*. This chromolithograph was published in the *Gardeners' Chronicle* and was based on William Nesfield's drawing for one of the central parterres at Crewe Hall (1840-60). It shows his adaptation of various seventeenth-century motifs.

109. Castle Ashby, Northamptonshire. A veritable extravaganza of Victorian bedding laid out by the 4th Marquess of Northampton in the mid nineteenth century. The photograph is by *Country Life*, 1898.

sought for by gentleman of taste in every part of the country'.

Donald Beaton, the well known Victorian horticulturist, commented in the *Cottage Gardener* (28 October 1852, page 67) on some 'tracings of a flower garden' which he had been sent by William Nesfield and drew attention to what he called 'a new feature':

I mean his introducing Box as a *relief,* or green colour...This style is all but quite new in this country. I only know of a few places where box-beds, or beds of some flowerless plants are used; but on the Continent, I hear the plan is common, and I know that some old foreign authors treat of this style as quite familiar. The different coloured gravels, pebbles, and sand they use in Italy, in their Italian gardens, is part and parcel of the same; but here, with our moist climate, and our superabundance of half-hardy and fine-leaved plants, we need not resort to such extremes.

Despite this criticism in the gardening press of a style which Beaton saw as inappropriate for 'our moist climate', Nesfield's reputation grew, and he continued regularly to use coloured materials in his parterres as well as flowers. One of his earliest and most prestigious commissions was for the replanning of Kew Gardens in

the 1840s to develop a grand layout around the new palm house. He designed the terrace with its parterre and a seventeenth-century *patte d'oie* with vistas leading to the Pagoda, Syon House, and a mature Cedar of Lebanon. After that many commissions followed and one of the most extensive was for Crewe Hall, Cheshire, where he worked for over twenty years between 1840 and 1860. At Crewe his scheme for the parterre is typical of the kind for which he will be remembered (plate 108). His coloured drawing for the immense parterre shows his application to historical precedent and interpretation. The design includes a marvellous range of ornament – the guilloche plait around the top reminiscent of those early Roman mosaics, a great palm leaf in the centre, floral arabesques picking their way over the centre ground, and the whole framed with bands of colour and box edging. It seems he wanted the parterre to be as artificial as possible – an aim which is quite in sympathy with a seventeenth-century approach.

Nesfield's attention to detail was almost excessive and no colour or gradation of colour went without considerable thought as to how it was going to look on the ground from the main rooms of the house. There is a most enlightening documentation and correspondence about the parterre at Stoke Edith, home of the Foley family, which reveals Nesfield's intentions (plate 110). Next to an early sketch for the parterre he wrote about his concern for the appearance of the long beds that form the scrolls 'where the deepest scarlet commences at the circle A & blends imperceptibly towards B into orangy red & thence towards C into salmon red'. He wanted to keep the darkest colours near the house and the paler at the far end, with increasing amounts of green, so that the parterre could 'blend' with the parkland beyond. Lady Foley was concerned about the scrollwork compartments and in a letter to Nesfield she complained that the embroidery was 'too delicate for the Park scenery as a background'. Nesfield in reply resorts to a musical analogy:

Some few lines are intentionally single... acting with others on a graduated scale as the octaves in musical chords – in fact they constitute the charm of good composition in as much as they not only produce 'Variety' but give energy to all the broader lines which are Bass notes – This comes under the head of 'Proportion' upon which important quality a celebrated Artistical Author says 'Proportion is to form what time is to music, or measure to Poetry'. (from Christopher Ridgway, a case study from the Nesfield Conference, IAA S, at York in 1994)

Nesfield carried out over 200 successful commissions in his lifetime, but attitudes to garden design changed in the late nineteenth century and his work, and the popularity of the French style parterre in particular, suffered. Part of the cause was no doubt the expensive upkeep of such large scale projects. They required huge maintenance if they were to be kept in the way they were planned. The parterres at Stoke Edith and Crewe have both been lost, but one of the rare survivals is the one designed for Sir Charles Tempest at Broughton Hall, North Yorkshire, between 1855 and 1857 (although at least one parterre was grassed over and replanted at the turn of the century). The large parterre on sloping ground to the east of the house is ideally situated for viewing from the upper rooms (plate 112). It was created with scrolls and feather plumes in box, and coloured gravels were used in the spaces – a practice Nesfield often employed and which of course

110. Stoke Edith, Herefordshire. William Nesfield's striking parterre design of the 1850s was still in good shape at the time this photograph was taken in about 1900.

had its precedent in the French parterre, particularly in the work of John James. A fascinating letter in the archives at Broughton draws attention to Nesfield's difficulties in finding suitable coloured materials for the parterre and also reflects on his work at Stoke Edith:

When last I had the pleasure of visiting Broughton, you mentioned knowing of some quarry in your neighbourhood affording an agreeable blue colour which I did not notice sufficiently at that time in consequence of having several

111, 112 and 113. Broughton Hall, Yorkshire. William Nesfield's large parterre (c. 1855) is sited on rising ground so that the pattern can be ideally viewed from the upper floors and roof. Traces of the blue spar can still be seen between the hedges at the far end. Another parterre at Broughton lies in front of the original conservatory of 1834. In the photograph (below) taken early this century, Nesfield's parterre is in the background.

specimens of blue & other colours of *artificial gravel* with me (which were shown to you & Miss Tempest as top dressings to the gravel alleys of the proposed parterres) – now it appears these materials contain *lead* which is *poisonous* to vegetation. A letter of this morning from Lady Emily Foley states that the *blue* sent by my order to her had killed the box which annoys me much. (quoted from Brent Elliott, *Victorian Gardens*, 1986)

There is another magnificent Nesfield parterre of the 1850s on the terrace at Holkham Hall in Norfolk, and one of his maze designs, an aspect of garden layout which Thomas Hill treated alongside the knot garden, still exists at Somerleyton, also in Norfolk. Nesfield's use of monograms, carried out with great effect at Crewe Hall, became a central feature of his later work and is another link with the Tudor period when the use of interlaced initials and coats of arms was an important feature of the gardens. At Bodrhyddan, Denbighshire, his son W.E.Nesfield added an elaborate parterre in 1873-74, sometimes called the 'Dutch' parterre.

One of Nesfield's later commissions was for the Avenue Gardens in Regent's Park in London which he began in 1863 and then collaborated on with his sons Eden and Markham Nesfield from 1864. The original conception was for an 'Avenue Garden' to be created within the centre of a four line avenue which had been planted at the beginning of the century. The scheme for an Italian garden with a geometric bedding scheme with vases, pedestals, and a tazza supported by griffins, was not entirely greeted with approval in the editorial of the *Gardeners' Chronicle* (15 August 1863) which commented that it was no longer possible to enjoy the 'leafy avenues as of yore' and that the visitor had to endure 'the glaring expanse of hot and dusty or shingly gravel' and 'beds of blazing flowers and plantations of fancy shrubs'. But within a year approval was forthcoming and the gardens were extended, with Markham Nesfield becoming more involved and advising on a planting scheme for the eastern side of the avenue in the form of two tapering beds of a guilloche pattern. For the next twenty years the gardens were well maintained (as described in Cole's *Royal Parks,* 1877), but they were in decline by 1900, and during the course of this century had become almost unrecognisable. However a decision was taken to restore the Nesfield gardens; work began in 1992 and was completed in 1995 (plates 114-16).

In social and political terms the nineteenth century began to change after the financial crisis in the 1870s, and country house gardens on the scale of the 1850s began to decline. Also the Art Workers' Guild was formed in 1884, becoming the centre of the Arts and Crafts movement, and although there is no direct connection between these events, attitudes to gardens and garden making were shortly to change. However an article in the *Journal of Horticulture and Cottage Gardener* in 1874 referring to Thomas Hill's *Gardeners Labyrinth* was still disparaging about early practices, 'It contains more woodcuts of the flower knots, rude precedents of our bedding out' (page 449). Clearly the popular gardening press of the day still saw early forms of garden design as raw and primitive when compared with the highly

skilled bedding schemes of the 1870s which, along with carpet bedding (the practice of using low-growing plants to make a pattern like a carpet), had reached recognisably ridiculous levels of ingenuity. William Robinson, the well known garden writer and publisher, called them 'pastrycooks' gardens' – a comment that recalls Francis Bacon's, quoted earlier (page 54). He was one of the sternest critics of bedding schemes, advocating a new approach in *The Wild Garden* (1870) and later championing the virtues of the cottage garden.

Many others had led the way in reviving the 'old fashioned' garden – the books of E.V.Boyle (1825-1916) were persuasive of the virtues of early garden design, and she also began to reshape her own garden at Huntercombe Manor in Buckinghamshire in 1871 with yew hedges, pyramid yews and old fashioned plants, doing much to develop the trend which turned away from the gaudiness of Victorian bedding schemes. Lady Egerton at Hardwick Hall, Derbyshire, replanned the old walled garden to the south of the great house with lines of formal yews dividing the square into quarters, but few went so far as to revive the simple knot garden. The exceptions include Ludstone Hall in Shropshire, where Joseph Cartwright, who bought the property in

114, 115 and 116. The cable frieze flower beds in the Avenue Gardens in Regent's Park, London. The parterres have recently been extensively restored following the original plans by William and Markham Nesfield. A detail of William Nesfield's plan of 1863 is shown on the right.

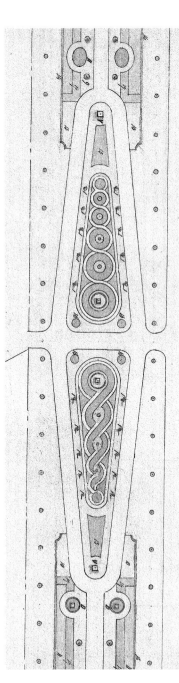

1870, planted a garden in keeping with the Jacobean manor and laid out a large knot in four squares, each divided into four quarters and all surrounding a central corkscrew of box. Two of the squares on the diagonal were composed of box cut into the shapes of spades, hearts, diamonds and clubs. At Amport in Hampshire the 14th Marquis of Winchester laid out a new garden in the 1860s including a knot garden in box and coloured gravel in the form of the family crest. Another 'old garden' that was created towards the end of the century is at Broughton Castle in Oxfordshire, where the enclosed area known as the Ladies' Garden next to the house has been designed with charming box edged fleur-de-lis, planted with roses, and circles with lavender (plate 118). Bodysgallen in North Wales has a fine parterre filled with herbs in a walled area below the house, surviving from the late nineteenth century (plate 119).

Englishness of course had been a key concern of the Arts and Crafts architects. One of them, John Dando Sedding (1838-91), a founding architect of the Guild, had written *Garden-Craft Old and New* (1891) in a mood of exultation to resurrect old English gardens in which he took national pride. He wanted to prove the worth of English gardens, 'that piece of hoarded loveliness', against foreign models. Reginald Blomfield came next with his immensely persuasive little book, *The Formal Garden,* with delightful woodcuts by Inigo Thomas illustrating old fashioned gardens and including illustrations of knot gardens gathered from various sources, including Hill, Surflet, Lawson and Markham. All would seem to have been set for a revival of the 'knot garden', but although Edwardian gardens showed much influ-

ence of 'Old England' (and 'Old Italy' for that matter) knot gardens *per se* did not make a revival in the form in which they had originally been conceived.

Many 'old fashioned' gardens were created with formal arrangements of quarters, cut yews and typically geometric box enclosures but none seem to have gone as far as to use interlacing hedges to make knots. Inigo Triggs's design for the garden at Athelhampton (1891-93) is an example, where superb pyramid yews surrounded small geometric beds, all arranged in quarters around a central fountain. A rather different approach was taken by Blomfield for the gardens at Mellerstain (1909), near Gordon on the Borders, where he laid out a French style parterre with fans cut in box and box compartments of roses and catmint on the

**118. Broughton Castle, Oxfordshire. A roof top view of the fleur-de-lis beds in the Ladies' Garden.**

**117 *left*. Ludstone Hall, Shropshire. Surviving from the late nineteenth century this 'old fashioned garden' was laid out in quarters, some with box cut into clubs, hearts, diamonds and spades, surrounding a central corkscrew of box.**

119. Bodysgallen, North Wales. The parterre, dating from the late nineteenth century, is well placed in its walled enclosure to be viewed from the terrace walk above.

terrace beneath the windows of the Adam House; all this in the best chateau tradition at the start of a long vista leading down to a formal lakeside (plate 120).

At Blenheim too, French influence is in evidence: Achille Duchêne (1866-1947), a French garden designer who had taken part in many of the classic restorations of magnificent seventeenth-century French gardens, was commissioned to design a *parterre de broderie* on the east front (the Italian garden) and the grand water parterre on the west (completed by 1930) with baroque arabesques making up the water basin surrounded by complementary box parterres of scrolls and cartouches with gravel in between (plate 100). The design owes much to the complex form of the *parterre d'eau* at Versailles.

If one is trying to trace the revival of the knot garden, in the strict sense, in the late nineteenth century and the early years of the twentieth century, then Henry Ellacombe and Ernest Law are the key figures. Canon Ellacombe (1822-1916), one of the leading players on the horticultural stage in the 1880s and 1890s, wrote two now very familiar books: *Plant-lore and Garden-craft of Shakespeare* (1878), which went through a number of editions by the end of the century, and *In a Gloucestershire Garden* (1895), which was reflections on his garden at Bitton in Gloucestershire. It was the first book which provoked a fashion for 'Shakespeare's garden' and stimulated a keen interest in the flowers of Tudor England. These 'notes', as Ellacombe called them in his preface to the first edition, were first published in *The Garden* in 1877 and drew his readers' attention to the 'great feature of the Elizabethan garden', the formation of the 'curious knotted gardens':

Each of the large compartments was divided into a complication of 'knots' by which was meant beds arranged in quaint patterns, formed by rule and compass with mathematical precision, and so numerous that it was a necessary part of the system that the whole square should be fully occupied by them... The 'knots' were generally raised above the surface of the paths, the earth being kept in its place by borders of lead, or tiles, or wood, or even bones; but sometimes the beds and paths were on the same level, and then there were the same edgings that we now use, as Thrift, Box, Ivy, flints, etc.

It seems he was not entirely happy with the idea of knots, which he calls 'quaint', and his use of box and ivy for edgings is characteristic of Victorian taste rather than historically accurate. He continued:

I doubt not that the efficiency of an Elizabethan gardener was as much tested by his skill and experience in "knot-work," as the efficiency of a modern gardener is tested by his skill in "bedding out," which is the lineal descendant of "knot-work"...Such was the Elizabethan garden in its general outlines.

He concluded that 'the whole fashion of the Elizabethan garden has passed away, and will probably never be revived', and in spite of pointing out how successful this style of gardening had been for 200 years, he just about dismissed it as completely 'ridiculous', and said that none of us would want to abandon 'our winding walks and undulating lawns' for 'the straight walks and level terraces of the sixteenth century' (2nd edition, 1884, page 348).

Despite Ellacombe's leanings towards the Robinsonian 'natural' approach to garden design, interest in recreating the Tudor garden was taken up by Ernest Law (1854-1930) who wrote a comprehensive history of Hampton Court (3 vols, 1885-91) and recreated Shakespeare's garden at New Place, Stratford-on-Avon (1919-21), which he later claimed 'was the first knott-garden

**120. Mellerstain, Borders Region. Reginald Blomfield's French style parterre of 1909 lies below the house at the head of the long vista leading down to the lake.**

121. New Place, Stratford-on-Avon. Here Ernest Law recreated 'Shakespeare's garden' and today it is filled with bright and colourful flowers. Such a spectacle would not have been possible in Shakespeare's day.

ever made in England since the time of the early Stuarts' (plate 121). He went on to say that the Elizabethan knot garden at Hampton Court, with plans printed in his illustrated guide *Hampton Court Gardens* (1926), was the second and described the source of the designs: 'The patterns of the interlacing bands or "ribbons" are taken entirely from those designed and published by the old masters on gardening of the time of Elizabeth and James I' (plate 134). Comparison of these designs with those in Hill and others shows that Law only used the original designs as a basis for his own; on three points at least he has departed from Elizabethan precedents: none of his designs are based on the square, all contain lavender and box, and two of the designs have ovals at their centres. In the 1926 guide he shows his nostalgia

for 'simple old English' names, as opposed to the Latin ones, when he says: 'How one hates these horrid, absurd, uncouth Latin names, which convey nothing to most people, and which few can pronounce, but which these high-brow botanists are trying to force on simple-speaking gardeners and lovers of gardens!'. It is such personal sentiments as these which probably detracted from general enthusiasm for 'quaint' Elizabethan gardens, and in the 1920s the spirit of modernism began to lead the way forward, with garden design turning its back on the past and ignoring revivalism, which had been so stimulated by the Arts and Crafts architects at the end of the Victorian era.

It is in the second half of the twentieth century that the passion for the conservation and restoration of Brit-

122. Ditchley Park, Oxfordshire. The twentieth-century parterre was designed by Geoffrey Jellicoe in 1936 for Ronald and Nancy Tree. It shows perfect French elegance and symmetry.

ain's heritage has led the way in the preservation and restoration of existing historic gardens and the recreation of many that had been lost. The formation of bodies like the Garden History Society in 1965, more recently the various county trusts for gardens, and the Welsh Historic Gardens Trust, have stimulated our awareness of landscape history. Publications too have blossomed, and some like *Discovering Period Gardens* (Shire 1972) were early signposts to historic gardens. Since then many histories of gardens have been written, and these too have channelled people's energies in the direction of restoration. The particular search for the formal garden before 1700 has led to a deepening familiarity with the detailed aspects of such designs, and the 'knot garden' has often been the key element in the restoration.

Some enlightened approaches were undertaken before 1950; a shining example is Edzell Castle in Scotland where the basic structure of Sir David Lindsay's castle and the remarkable walled garden of 1604 survived and provided a marvellous opportunity for the recreation of the pleasance (plate 123). The state took over the site in 1932 and without any archaeological evidence of the layout, plans for 'knots' to 'restore' an early seventeenth-century garden were prepared with the work

mainly being executed during the 1930s. Today some would criticise the historical accuracy of such an undertaking, particularly in its planting, but at the time it was constructed it was the first of its kind and little attention had then been focused on the details of such gardens. Another early pioneer project was Kirby Hall in Northamptonshire. In 1935 it became the scene of the first recorded excavation of a garden in an attempt to rediscover the great formal gardens that the fourth Sir Christopher Hatton had laid out in 1685-86; since then further archaeological investigation has taken place in the 1980s with the intention of restoring these early gardens. Leading projects after 1950 have been Pitmedden in Scotland, which was given to the National Trust in 1952, and where restoration of the parterres followed in the same decade (plate 97), the parterre for the Queen's Garden at Kew which was opened in 1969, the seventeenth-century parterre at Little Moreton in 1972 (plate 88), the Tudor Garden created by Sylvia Landsberg at the Tudor House Museum, Southampton, in the late 1970s (plate 40), the knot gardens at St Fagans Castle, Cardiff, and a number of others since.

Rosemary Verey has been one of the foremost in the study of knot gardens. She compiled a bibliography of

123 *right*. Edzell Castle, Tayside. This rare survival of an early walled garden, dated 1604, is one of the earliest examples of a recreated garden. The box design, motto and other motifs were all completed by the end of the 1930s.

sources for the Garden History Society's journal in 1974 and about that time planted an authentic knot garden at Barnsley House in Gloucestershire (plate 140) using a design from Markham and the 'True Lovers Knott' from Stephen Blake's *The Compleat Gardeners Practice* (1664). The 1970s must have been a particularly active period for recreations of the knot garden: one made its appearance at thé Chelsea Flower Show in an exhibition on the history of the garden by Reading University, and also in 1970 the Plymouth Barbican Association laid out an Elizabethan garden, which included knots, in commemoration of the 350th anniversary of the departure of the Mayflower. More recently in 1983 the Garden History Society held a symposium on the knot garden, which included a visit to the West Garden at Hatfield House where they were shown the new knot gardens designed by the Marchioness of Salisbury.

In twentieth-century Britain the parterre has enjoyed more favour amongst designers than the knot. An outstanding example was designed at Ditchley Park, Oxfordshire by Geoffrey Jellicoe in 1936 for the Americans, Ronald and Nancy Tree (plate 122). Nevertheless, until recently, garden formality has not been enthusiastically embraced by designers, so examples of the parterre made in this century in Britain are rare.

On looking abroad it is evident too that the knot garden in its original form has remained a particularly European garden feature and if it can be said to have enjoyed a revival in the twentieth century there seems little sign that this characteristic garden motif has spread to other parts of the world, except under the influence of very recent landscape designers. The situation in America at the end of the nineteenth century reflects some of the most lavish European examples at the time. The new industrial American millionaires were building immense houses using European styles and surrounding them, as the Victorians had done in Britain, with magnificent gardens; there began what has been called 'the golden age of American gardens, 1890-1940'. The French parterre was recreated in the New World by Jacques Greber, a distinguished French garden designer, who was brought over to America in the early years of this century specifically to introduce this style of gardening. A fine example of his work was created early

this century at Harbour Hill, Long Island, below the windows of a new French chateau. Another by Greber was at Miramar on Rhode Island where he laid out a grand *parterre de broderie* in the best seventeenth-century style. The Americans at this time echoed the Victorian love of brightly coloured bedding schemes and it is said that in the 1880s the Philadelphia millionaire Fairman Rogers threw a Persian carpet on the lawn and asked his gardener to duplicate the effect; it is reported that it needed over 3000 plants to do so (Mac Griswold and Eleanor Weller, *The Golden Age of American Gardens*). In spite of this enthusiasm for patterned gardens the knot garden as such was not taken up in America at this time. However it seems inconceivable that the early settlers did not use box to surround their beds, and if the recreation of George Washington's garden at The American Museum in Britain (Claverton Manor, near Bath) gives us an idea of the kind of garden created by the early settlers then box compartments were certainly used.

It may seem rather perverse to discuss the distinction between the knot garden and the parterre in the concluding chapter of a book on the history of the subject. It will be apparent by now though that there are great difficulties in trying to reach a flawless distinction between the two because in most cases it is the historical context of the words which is more important than the visual form. The point has been made a number of times that 'parterre' is synonymous with 'flower garden', whereas 'knot', in its strictest sense, implies the apparent weaving together of low growing hedges, and that historically the knot garden belongs to the Tudor period. Its defining qualities are scale and form – it is generally of a modest size, based on the square, usually symbolic or emblematic and the design is made with herbs, but excludes box. The parterre on the other hand, a word of course borrowed from the French, came into fashion in the seventeenth century and its defining characteristics are its tendency to be large, a preference for the long rectangle (to take advantage of perspective as Stephen Switzer explains in *Ichnographia Rustica*, 1718), emphasis on decorative elements (embroidered shapes, fans, palms, cartouches, etc.) rather than symbolic, and the ubiquitous use of box compartments, cut turf (*gazon coupé*), and coloured infils (gravel, sand,

**124. The knot garden designed by Johnny Woodford for Bryan and Angela Hunt shows that the 1990s knot may take more from Celtic art than from the long tradition of knot gardens and parterres that began with the gardens of the Tudors.**

chippings, etc). In the nineteenth century the regular use of the word parterre to describe various forms of pattern gardening has the effect of broadening the definition further. For the purists 'knot' can only really be applied to conscious attempts to recreate Tudor knot gardens; all the rest are best considered as parterres.

Also it has been noticeable over the last twenty years that the vagaries of fashion (or perhaps an increased awareness of historical correctness) have exerted their influence on the use of the two words. Twenty years ago, among the *cognoscenti* knot gardens had been 'discovered' and were mainly devised with patterns of box hedges and compartments filled in with colourful plants and herbs. More recently, and in retro-

spect, doubt has crept in as to the suitability of applying this term when it transpires that box was not recommended at all for Tudor knots. Suddenly what were happily 'knot gardens' have now turned into parterres. Dare it be suggested that once again French words have ousted good common English?

Let those who enjoy the practical aspects of knot gardens be not troubled by these ruminations and quibbles, but rather proceed to take on board a wide range of designs so that in the second part of this book practical aspects can be pursued without the constraint of definitions. As Parkinson says: 'Let every man therefore, if hee like of these, take what may please his mind, or out of these or his own conceit, frame any other to his fancy'.

PART TWO

# HOW TO MAKE YOUR OWN KNOT GARDEN

ANNE JENNINGS

125. A roof top view of the knot garden at the
Museum of Garden History

# ELEMENTS OF DESIGN

## INTRODUCTION

My interest in knot gardens began some years ago when I was lucky enough to be appointed Garden Director at The Museum of Garden History. In 1981 a replica seventeenth-century knot, designed by Lady Salisbury, had been planted and I was to be responsible for its care and development. With the help of hard working volunteers, the knot remains one of the best examples of its type and contains a wide range of plants which were grown in Britain during the seventeenth century. Any dedicated gardener who cares for a garden in a practical way almost inevitably becomes attached to it and before long I had grown to love this small but valuable treasure.

At first I only visited the garden once a week, but each time I would find another surprise. In the cold of winter I would pause to appreciate the intricacies of the hedge pattern. In summer I had hardly time to notice one newly opened flower before another beckoned. This small garden epitomises everything which excites and stimulates me as a gardener. From the combination of formal design softened by exuberant planting to the guarantee of year round interest, the knot garden inspires me as a designer, a gardener and a romantic.

The strongest aesthetic feature of a knot garden is the blend of geometry with plants, creating patterns to please the eye and calm the spirit. This was certainly recognised by earlier gardeners like Thomas Hill who considered the patterns to be 'for the comfort and delight of his wearied mind'. The design itself can either be simple and stylised with the pattern of low hedges emphasised by gravel filled compartments – ideal for small sites, perhaps courtyards or urban gar-

dens. Alternatively the strong underlying structure of the hedge can combine with soft internal planting. In summer this will have the informal disorganised beauty of a cottage garden but in winter the exposed pattern of the knot is dramatic in its simplicity. It is this flexibility which gives knot gardens such potential today.

Drawing inspiration only from historical gardens is often criticised by contemporary designers. Imitation or pastiche can lack creativity and today's designers do well to embrace modern concepts and materials. However, the wealth of artistry and skill uncovered during the study of garden history is too great to be ignored; to do so would be to waste a valuable resource. Certain situations do demand an authentic reproduction of a particular style, but there are plenty of opportunities to create new gardens powerfully influenced by the past but with a contemporary appearance and character. Lady Salisbury's knot gardens at Hatfield House are an inspiration to us all.

Images and patterns that have been or could be used for knot garden design are reproduced throughout the first part of this book and I find their symmetry and balance irresistible. There is an addictive pleasure in developing the designs on paper with the ambition of making a garden. Designing a knot is a good introduction to garden design as you work within a strong framework that almost naturally develops into a balanced pattern. With simple drawing tools, anyone can integrate lines and circles to make beautiful patterns and those with more confidence can design freehand, perhaps in the style of a calligrapher or embroiderer. Once you become aware of patterns suitable for knot garden design you will see potential at every turn. It is worth remembering that

knots can be used for memorials or celebratory gardens, as initials, emblems or symbols can be incorporated to personalise or add intrigue to the design.

Creating any new garden is an exciting experience; the gardener is like an artist transforming his blank canvas into a masterpiece and perhaps more than any other garden style, the knot garden is the one that allows its maker the widest range of colour, texture and shape. A crucial element in creating this three-dimensional work of art is effective planting and it is with planting that I begin. You will find full instructions for design, planting plan, ground preparation, setting out the design on the site and future care and maintenance between pages 140 and 155. Whether you are planting a simple knot with gravel filled compartments or a fully planted version over-

flowing with flowers, you will be guided step by step.

I hope you will find all the practical advice and creative stimulus you need to design your own knot. A list of knot gardens and parterres open to the public is on page 156 and a visit to any will be an inspiration. If possible visit more than once to see the garden in different seasons. My own experience caring for the knot at the Museum has brought me enormous pleasure and I do hope I can convey some of my own enthusiasm. Ours is not an easy garden to care for, existing as it does in traffic-polluted London. The soil is poor, financial resources are limited and gardeners work only part time. Despite these and other difficulties, the garden gives pleasure to many visitors each year and is the inspiration behind my courses and this part of the book.

**127. Lady Salisbury's East Garden at Hatfield House is a parterre on a grand scale. Inside the box hedge roses and herbaceous plants flourish informally throughout the year.**

**126** *previous page.* **The knot at the Museum of Garden History in Lambeth. The reproduction seventeenth-century knot garden designed by Lady Salisbury and looked after by Anne Jennings is both a delightful haven and a mine of information about plant introductions.**

**128. The Knot Garden, Hatfield House. Here the intimacy of the knot garden belies the scale and grandeur of the Old Palace against which it is set.**

## SIZE, SETTING AND STYLE

Whether you own acres of land in the country or a small back yard in the city, a knot can be designed to suit the size and situation of your garden. From elaborate, sweeping parterres to tiny, detailed knots, the gardens are flexible, not only in size but also style. I use 'knot garden' as an umbrella term because clear definitions between a knot and parterre are, as we have seen, difficult to establish and need not concern us here.

In its simplest, unplanted form a knot can be made on the smallest site. Small gardens can be treasures and while acres of land may disguise design errors or maintenance problems, every corner of a small garden is available for scrutiny and inspection. Simple designs are most effective in small spaces and a square or circle measuring only 1 metre across could be planted with box to enclose a bay tree, clipped to a lollipop shape. With a little more space, perhaps 2 metres long and 1 metre wide, a rectangle enclosing a latticework pattern of hedging could be made. These

elegant gardens would demand minimum maintenance as the hedge would need cutting only once or twice a year. With a little extra work, the knot could be decorated with seasonal bulbs, perhaps tulips in spring and agapanthus or lilies in summer. Bulbs can be planted direct into the ground or pots could be placed in compartments, lifted and replaced as necessary. As a general rule, internal compartments should be no smaller than the width of the hedge, around 30 cm, to ensure the pattern does not disappear as the hedge matures.

The smallest knot garden I know is made in a clover leaf shaped bowl, measuring about 75 cm across. The owner fills the bowl with compost and plants cuttings of box and other shrubs in patterns, like miniature hedges. The cuttings root *in situ* and can be lightly clipped for two or three years before

**129** *left*. An elegant parterre by the garden designer Paul Miles. A newly planted yew hedge gives the parterre its boundary and the design cleverly incorporates a lovely mature tree.

**130** *left below*. A tiny, low growing knot also by Paul Miles. The knot is less than 3 metres square and planted with a carpet of creeping herbs and alpines.

**131.** A London basement: a fine solution for a difficult site.

being potted on, then the process begins again. This delightful little garden stands on a pedestal, raising the plants to chest level so the knot can be seen in all its intricate detail.

Large gardens can incorporate knots by enclosing them with hedges or screens, but they can also be made on a terrace or wide front lawn. Scale and proportion are important considerations to ensure the garden creates dramatic effect in a bigger landscape; generosity in shape, size and design are needed. Intricate curls and patterns are effective in a traditional parterre, especially if a double row of plants are used for a wider hedge. Alternatively, the pattern could be simpler but incorporate compartments for dramatic planting, such as the East Garden at Hatfield House where Scotch thistle, *Onopordum acanthium* and the tree poppy, *Romneya coulteri*, are grown. In extremely large areas, a series of knots, perhaps a block of four, each measuring 10 metres square would be more successful than one enormous garden. The designs could either be identical or a series of different patterns to complement one another. Topiary, arbours, pergolas and wide paths can all be a part of the large parterre; the style offers few limitations although cost may well have a restraining effect on ambition.

As interest in garden history and design has grown, so there have been many restorations and recreations, several incorporating knot gardens and parterres. Lady Salisbury's design for the Museum was inspired by Thomas Hill's writings and plans. The pattern, less than nine metres square, incorporates circles and squares with the letter 'T' for Tradescant repeated symmetrically throughout the design. Dwarf box, *Buxus sempervirens* 'Suffruticosa', forms the main hedge with *Santolina chamaecyparissus*, cotton lavender, making the T shapes. Another striking knot was designed by Sylvia Landsberg for Tudor House in Southampton in the early 1980s (see plate 40). If you are the owner of a sixteenth-century home, you might well want to recreate a garden in this style, but knots can be used in a much wider context and associate well with a range of architectural styles.

A parterre in front of a modern terrace house would be visually exciting. It would also make a horticultural statement for owners who shunned the predictability of the handkerchief-sized lawn, choosing instead a garden which epitomised style and simplicity. Rambling roses and other cottage elements may be unsuitable for the facade of a 1970s building with strong lines and large areas of glass. Instead the complementary restraint of a knot would create harmony between house and garden. I often work in city gardens, surrounded by tall buildings and heavily shaded by large trees and walls. Here flowers reach for the light, gangly and awkward in their search for the sun; shrubs are bare at the base, covered with leaves only on the uppermost branches and climbing plants scramble above the eye line searching for light. A knot planted with box would survive happily in such environments, remaining thick and green in dense or dappled shade.

Knot gardens can be designed in so many different styles it is difficult to imagine one could not be made to suit any horticultural taste. During the early stages of drawing the design, your choice of patterns and shapes will influence style; whether the garden will have a traditional or contemporary feel, whether one or more plant varieties will be used for the hedge and how large the internal compartments are to be. The relationship between house and garden will also

**132. Rousham House, Oxfordshire. Roses contrast with the clipped hedge of the parterre set in front of the beautiful pigeon house.**

**133 *right*. On a raised terrace at one end of a country garden a delightful design based on a Valentine's card. The four knots alternate intertwined hearts and initial letters. The seat and clipped dome of lavender provide a focus to the design and there is an intimate feel to this private garden within the larger Suffolk landscape.**

**134 and 135** *following page*. **The simple 'Tudor Knot' at Hampton Court Palace, with compartments filled with bedding plants, contrasts with the dramatic scale and setting of the Lutyens/Jekyll 'Great Plat' at Hestercombe in Somerset where** *Bergenia cordifolia* **replaces formal hedges.**

be important and you need to consider how it will be viewed. If you can see your knot from above, perhaps through a bedroom window, design it to take advantage of the elevated view, using different hedge plants to weave intricate patterns. If the garden is only seen at ground level, you may decide on a simpler design and create additional interest with topiary, water fountains or statuary.

Another essential feature which will dictate the style of the garden is the path. The knot at the Museum is surrounded by a path so the garden is only viewed from the outside. This creates an inward looking garden, appropriate for our site as the views

beyond the boundaries are unexciting. Additionally, 1000 visitors each week cause no damage to the internal planting as they are unable to enter the knot. With more space and an attractive surrounding landscape, the knot could be dramatically different in style if the paths dissected it, inviting close inspection of plants. It is also important to think of the central focal point in both situations. The spiral of variegated holly at the centre of the Museum knot emphasises the inward looking nature of the site, drawing the eye to the middle of the garden. With paths running through the design you may decide to make a central seating area, looking out into the garden beyond.

One of the most important effects on knot garden style is planting. From the simplicity of the unplanted knot, dependent on pattern and structure for interest, to the flamboyance of cottage style planting, the knot or parterre can adopt many different characters. Intricate hedge patterns tend to leave small internal compartments, so the knot might remain unplanted or be used for simple seasonal interest, such as bulbs. When the pattern creates large compartments, other planting styles can be used; topiary, rose or herb gardens, bedding schemes and colour co-ordinated planting can set the theme. Gardening books and magazines are a constant source of inspiration for planting ideas, and schemes intended for borders can often be adapted to suit a knot. Again, I strongly recommend visiting gardens; take a book and note your favourite plants or combinations. If you want to make an unplanted knot, Rosemary Verey's is one of the best (plate 140), and if you are keen on vegetables, her potager shows how well box hedging and vegetables combine.

By this stage you will be eager to design your knot and should know where it will be positioned and how much space is available. Perhaps you have already decided the planting style and have a clear idea of the basic pattern, but it is worth pausing a while to think about why you want to make a knot garden. Is historical accuracy in design and planting important? Perhaps you have an interest in the culinary, medicinal and aromatic uses of herbs or want to make an ornamental vegetable garden in the style of a parterre? You may spend long periods away from home so low maintenance is important as well as seasonal interest. All these considerations play an important part in the design process and it is worth spending time thinking and planning.

## HARD LANDSCAPING

Paths and other hard surfaces or structures are known as 'hard landscaping' as opposed to the 'soft landscaping' provided by plants. Hard landscaping can be one of the most expensive elements of a new garden and must be appropriate in style and material to create a feeling of harmony.

Medieval gardens were enclosed by small walls, palings or wattle fences with arbours, turf seats and trellis for decoration and practical use. Galleries, pavilions and canals were all detailed in Du Cerceau's drawings of sixteenth-century knot gardens and any of these features can be copied or used to inspire designs for a modern knot. In a small garden hard landscaping demands careful design to ensure materials, size and detail justify close inspection.

Unless your knot is in the style of a seventeenth-century parterre, designed for a large open lawn or terrace, you may wish to enclose it with some form of boundary. In an urban area you may be surrounded on all sides by other gardens, with a patchwork of different fence panels. Whatever your situation, it is important to ensure boundaries are decorative and complementary to the knot garden.

Walls can create heavy shade and dry areas of ground, but I would love a wall around my garden. Fitted with taut horizontal wires it could support espaliered fruit, roses and wall shrubs. New brick walls can be very expensive, but cheaper ones can be made from concrete blocks, then rendered and perhaps painted. An ideal height is around two metres, providing adequate support for climbing plants but not giving the garden the appearance of a fortress. If you prefer a light screen, upright iron posts can be used to support pleached lime or horn-beam. The borders beneath the trees can be unplanted or used for a billowing hedge of lavender, roses or other plants.

**136. Hard landscaping at Hatfield House. The structural quality of stone paving, statuary and the water fountain are a lovely contrast to the unmown meadow at the entrance to the Hatfield knot garden.**

We have already considered the importance of paths and how they influence the style of a garden. Gardeners have never had such a wide choice of paving materials. Natural stone remains expensive and its excavation causes irreparable harm to parts of the countryside. There are many reconstituted materials on the market and some are very good copies.

In general stone and imitation products are large materials where slabs might be 60 cm and more across. These may be disproportionate to the width of the path in a small knot garden where small unit paving such as bricks are more suitable. Clay bricks have a pleasing shape, texture and colour and reclaimed material looks attractively rustic. Bricks are designed

to create a vertical surface where water runs freely down the face of a wall. When they are used for paving water soaks into the brick and in cold areas the freeze-thaw effect will eventually cause the surface to spall and break away. I like this and think the rustic appearance suits many gardens, but others may prefer a cleaner surface. Concrete bricks or pavers are cheap and easy to lay and could be substituted but they lack much of the tactile quality of clay bricks.

Gravel is a suitable and cheap material for paths but it can be a nuisance and look untidy if it is laid loose where it can spill on to borders or lawns. If you want a loose gravel path, make sure you use an edging material such as timber, bricks or tiles, set slightly

higher than the finished level of the path to retain the gravel. Plastic or glass fibre landscape fabric can be laid as a membrane between the soil and the gravel, allowing rainwater to percolate, but preventing the soil from contaminating the gravel. The fabric also suppresses weeds to some extent.

The cheapest form of gravel is pea shingle, readily available from builders merchants in a pleasing combination of colours. Stone chippings are an alternative. These tend to be more expensive, angular rather than round and available in a range of stone types and colours. Loose materials can be combined with a weak mix of sand and cement and rolled or compacted with a vibrating plate to create a firmer surface. A natural alternative called 'self binding gravel' is also available. This is quarried gravel with a high clay content which acts as a binding agent and compacts to a firm surface when rolled. It looks good although it can be slightly dusty in summer and hold clay stained water in winter.

The possibilities for incorporating water into a knot garden are exciting and challenging. Formal pools, spouting jets, or trickling streams transform any garden by contributing sound and reflection. Air quality is improved in hot situations as water cools and refreshes the atmosphere. Box associates particularly well with water and topiary can be used effectively to reflect on the surface of a formal pool. Canals or rills can border a knot or run through the centre of a parterre and the channel can be lined with a range of attractive materials including tiles, paint or shining steel products to mimic mirrors.

Small areas of intense detail work effectively in enclosed situations. A pebble and tile mosaic edging the knot garden or a delicate band of shells collected from family holidays would contribute an element of individuality to any design. Statuary should be chosen carefully, ensuring the piece complements the size of the garden as well as the character, age and style of house. Containers or urns overflowing with seasonal plants can be strategically placed within a knot or parterre and are dramatic when incorporated into the design so that the hedge sweeps around the pot, enclosing it in a circle of permanent planting.

**138. A brickwork path in the Knot Garden at Hatfield. The bricks are laid in stretcher bond which is a very directional pattern emphasising the long, straight and narrow route.**

**139** *right*. **The Knot Garden, Sudeley Castle, Gloucestershire. The design is based on Princess Elizabeth's embroidered dress as seen in a painting hanging in the castle. There is also a Persian influence in the use of tile mosaics and water.**

# PLANTS FOR YOUR KNOT

Having thought about where you want to site your knot garden and what style you might choose, it is time to start making the choice of plants for the new garden. You may prefer to rely on the hedge pattern alone for interest, but if you decide to go for the fully planted version the choice of plants can be awe-inspiring. The next pages should help you distinguish between types of plants and how to use them.

Some garden owners pay contractors to carry out general maintenance work each week. In the badly ordered garden fees paid to professionals may be wasted as little impact can be made in the chaos of a poorly planted border, but good design and well thought out planting schemes can resolve such problems. Conversely, when the garden is cared for by an addicted gardener, it can flourish and transform itself. Roses, seasonal bulbs, hardy annuals, non-vigorous perennials, topiary and herbs all have a place in the plant lover's knot garden. For the dedicated gardener this is a blank canvas waiting to be filled with a wonderful array of flowering plants.

Plants to decorate internal compartments of a knot must be carefully chosen to ensure their own habit or vigour does not compete with the hedge. Annuals, biennials and perennials should either have strong, upright growth which will not swamp the hedge or they should be light and wafting in habit so that where they do rest, no damage is caused. Any ornamental hedge will suffer if dense, heavy plants rest against it for most of the growing season. At worst these areas will die back and require replacement.

Once the hedge is in place you will be keen to plant the whole of your knot garden as soon as possible, but it may be wise to put only the hedge and woody plants such as roses and topiary in place for

the first year or two. Some perennials can be extremely vigorous, growing quickly once spring arrives. If your hedge plants are small they may suffer harm from competitive neighbours so it may be worth delaying this planting for a couple of seasons to allow the hedge to establish itself before it has to compete for light, moisture and air.

We will take a seasonal look at plants, beginning with winter and focusing on the choice of hedge plants. The spring section is dominated by bulbs, but when we move into summer, the range of plants is enormous with annuals and biennials, perennials, summer bulbs and roses and climbers. Herbs and the potager come at the end.

## WINTER AND HEDGE PLANTS

In winter the main feature of the knot garden can be given in a word: hedges. It is the design of the hedge which creates focus and interest through the cold, grey months; perhaps most dramatically demonstrated when a layer of frost or a light covering of snow enhances geometry and pattern. It seems appropriate to begin by considering the species *Buxus*, or box, as today this is all but synonymous with knot gardens, even though we read that it was not originally used. References to its unpleasant smell suggest one possible reason for its unpopularity and box certainly has a strong scent; some people love it and others find it offensive, but in any case there is a deserved resurgence of interest in the plant, used either as hedging or for topiary.

I adore box hedges and am of course most intimate with the one at the Museum. Early summer is best of all, before the first cut. By this stage, vigorous

young shoots stand perhaps 12 cm high and include the most startling variety of shades of green. Our plants were purchased at the same time from the same source but even so there is an incredible variance in the colour of these young shoots. Once they mature a little and certainly after the first cut, this disappears and the hedge returns to a uniform colour, but at the time the display is as exciting as seeing a rainbow. Another reason for my obsession is the tactile appeal of the hedge. Before the first cut it develops a blancmange-like habit, billowing and bouncing at the slightest touch. Things tighten up a little after a disciplined haircut but the movement of the hedge at this time of year is delightful. At each corner of the knot, pyramids add height and structure to the design and after several years of training these have developed strong, upright growths. They are perhaps less responsive to touch than the rest of the hedge, but I cannot resist the occasional fond stroke.

It is important to distinguish between the numerous species and varieties of *Buxus* available throughout the world. There are large and small varieties, green, blue and gold forms, horizontal or upright habits as well as hardy and tender species. The European native *Buxus sempervirens* can grow into an immense plant, and the largest recorded planting of the species is at Birr Castle, Co. Offaly in Ireland where a 300 year old avenue of boxwood stands over eleven metres high.

The species can be trimmed regularly to keep it low and bushy, but a better choice for the knot garden is the variety 'Suffruticosa'. This has a naturally dwarf habit and will create a hedge up to 50 cm high although it can be trimmed lower if required. It has attractive, bright green foliage with fine textured leaves which help the plants to remain green and healthy even during dry, hot summers. In such conditions large leaved species can develop a bronze tinge

**141. Broughton Hall, Yorkshire. Cutting the hedge with round sides has exaggerated the swirling spiral pattern.**

**140** *previous page.* **The knot at Barnsley House, Gloucestershire, designed by Rosemary Verey is one of the best known knot gardens. It is an interpretation of Stephen Blake's 'True Lovers Knott' using dwarf box and wall germander for the weaving threads.**

**142. Little Moreton Hall, Cheshire. The gardener's break from hedge trimming gives a perfect example of before and after. It is an admirable hedge - dense right to the ground.**

to the foliage although this disappears once cooler, damp weather returns in autumn. Planting a dwarf variety reduces the number of cuts necessary each year; in a dry summer we only cut once in early May when the vigorous growth of spring has slowed. An earlier cut or a wet summer may necessitate a second cut in late August.

Planting distance depends slightly on time and budget available. Young plants set 15 cm apart will knit together to form a hedge within two or three years but such generous planting is expensive. Even 30 cm apart the plants will eventually knit together, although this will take several years and the resulting hedge may have a looser habit. Box plants can be bought as container grown specimens or as bare rooted stock for planting during the dormant season. Containerised plants are more expensive although timing is less crucial; a hedge can even be planted in summer if plants are carefully watered for the rest of

the season. The highly respected gardener Geoff Hamilton, who sadly died at the peak of his career, was a great advocate of economical gardening. He made a small knot garden in his ornamental vegetable garden and planted it with young plants which were taken as cuttings over several years from a few large specimens. As the young plants mature, they also offer material for cuttings and a cycle develops. If you are patient, or are planning a garden for the future, this is undeniably the least expensive way to plant a box hedge.

The traditional method of trimming a box hedge is to use hand shears, and it is good to watch a skilled gardener at work. It is crucial that the shears are held level and remain at the same height to ensure a clean, sharp line to the top of the hedge and less confident gardeners may find this difficult. Electric trimmers can be used and with care and experience a good finish can also be achieved. The machines are sharp and fast and unimaginable damage can be caused in seconds to the operator, hedge or internal planting. Herbaceous plants in compartments can easily be decapitated during a moment's lack of concentration. Always be aware of the danger of cutting the electric cable and use a power breaker. Protective trousers ensure the cutting teeth of the electric shears do not damage your legs – remember you may be standing in an awkward position when you are working inside the knot and good balance is crucial. After trimming, the top surface of the hedge may look brown for a couple of weeks but the rich green will return once damaged leaf edges have dropped.

*Buxus* is reliably long lived if trimmed regularly and cared for properly. When planting the hedge use a slow release, high phosphate fertiliser which can also be lightly forked into the top layer of soil each autumn. Avoid high nitrogen feeds in spring as these encourage vigorous leaf growth which may mean a second cut is necessary, but at this time of year apply a thick mulch to preserve moisture and keep roots cool during summer. New planting may require irrigation through the first season, but it is far better to ensure the ground is well prepared before planting to encourage roots to delve deep into the soil in search of moisture. Every three years or so the roots should be sliced to about a spade depth, approximately 15 cm either side of the central stem. This does no harm to the plant and in fact encourages the development of more fibrous roots.

Information about early knot gardens indicates that a wide variety of different plants were used to create hedges but some of these plants are not as popular for hedging today. However, it is interesting to consider some of these less common alternatives, perhaps resurrecting interest in their use.

Lavender is often seen forming a hedge at the front of an herbaceous border where it makes a billowing mound of silver foliage with flower spikes developing from July through to September. There are many forms of lavender which vary in hardiness and colour of both foliage and flowers although Old English Lavender, *Lavandula officinalis* (syn. *L. spica* and *L. angustifolia*) is the best known. Lavender will not make a strictly formal hedge as the flower spikes appear for perhaps four or five months of the year, disguising the strong architectural lines. Nevertheless, a simple knot planted with lavender would be a pleasant sight in the summer garden. The hedge would be trimmed to shape in late spring then clipped over to remove faded flower stems in late summer. Lavender can be short lived but is easy to propagate from cuttings to ensure plants are available as gap fillers.

Hyssop would form the same type of hedge as lavender, having a similar open habit and flowers on upright stems from July to September. Hedges can be cut back in late spring and faded flower stems removed as for lavender, but hyssop can also be trained as a very upright hedge if the sides are cut harder than the top in spring. Caroline Holmes used this technique in her knot garden at the Henry Doubleday Organic Gardens in Yalding, Kent and combined three varieties of hyssop to form weaving strands; *Hyssopus officinalis* with blue flowers, the pink form, *H.o.* 'Roseus' and the white flowered *H.o.* 'Albus'.

Rosemary makes an excellent hedge and if trimmed properly from an early age can last for many years. A 'little but often' trimming regime ensures a stocky, dense hedge although only an occasional bloom may develop on short stems. However, the scent which fills the air as aromatic oils are released during trimming compensates for lost flowers. A rosemary hedge surrounds one of the stone seats in the Museum garden and is now almost twenty years old. Occasional plants died and have been replaced but on the whole the hedge looks rather good. Until three years ago it was a traditional shape, with a flat top and straight sides but now it has developed into a rolling Chesterfield sofa.

The 'T' shapes in the Museum knot were originally planted with cotton lavender, *Santolina chamaecyparissus* (syn. *S. incana*). This is given a hard cut right back to the woody base each spring after the risk of frost has passed. The plants quickly regain

143. Tudor House, Southampton. The knot inspired by seventeenth-century designs uses box, cotton lavender, savory (*Satureja montana*) and germander (*Teuchrium chamaedrys*) to make the weaving hedges.

their height and once they reach the same level as the box hedge are given occasional light haircuts to keep them in shape. This is at the expense of flowers, but I prefer to grow cotton lavender for its foliage anyway. I particularly like two other forms, the green leaved *S. virens* and *S. neopolitana* with whiter grey leaves. Cotton lavender can look rather sparse and tatty through winter and occasionally plants may not survive very cold weather. *Santolina* cannot tolerate being used as a prop for other plants and sections of the hedge will die if softer plants lean against it. For

these reasons we have now decided to replace *Santolina* with *Helichrysum angustifolium,* curry plant, which clips in the same way. Both can be bought as small plants in the herb sections at garden centres, so make economical hedges. Use trimmings for cuttings to ensure you have replacements for dead plants.

Other woody herbs were used most effectively in sixteenth and seventeenth-century knot gardens for weaving under and over other species. Plants such as rue and winter savory have all been mentioned in early garden writing and contribute blue and dark

green leaves respectively. Germander is also referred to and this is most likely to be *Teucrium chamaedrys*, a hardy evergreen shrub with almost bottle green leaves and a grey underside. Lilac or pink flowers appear on spikes throughout summer and the plant should be trimmed as lavender. Another quite different variety is *T. fruticans*, a silver leaved plant with blue or lavender flowers from July to September. These appear on attractive white stems, shortened but still flowering when the plant is grown as a hedge. A two year old hedge at the Museum is proving a delight and thrives in a difficult situation

beneath *Robinia pseudoacacia*, where cotton lavender was miserable. Unfortunately *T. fruticans* is not reliably hardy although it suffers no problems in our mild garden. I have also seen it grown as a form of topiary, trained as a pyramid to great effect.

Many woody herbs develop a dense habit when trimmed regularly and although this is usually at the expense of the flowers, it offers an unusual way of growing common plants. Woody herbs such as forms of culinary sage, *Salvia officinalis,* are effective and the silver leaved curry plant, *Helichrysum angustifolium,* responds well to regular pruning. There are other

**144. Ham House, Richmond. There is a wonderful sculptural quality to this planting. Flat topped box hedges and cones contrast with hummocks of lavender and cotton lavender with the added bonus of deep green against blue grey.**

plants which could be used to create less traditional hedges, perhaps suitable for contemporary settings, for example:

*Berberis buxifolia* 'Nana'
*Caryopteris* x *clandonensis* 'Heavenly Blue'
*Euonymus fortunei* 'Emerald Gaiety'
*Hedera helix* 'Ivalace'
*Lonicera nitida*

In the first part of this book there are various mentions of soft or low growing plants forming the hedge in a knot and I am intrigued by the thought of using thyme, marjoram, chamomile or pennyroyal, a creeping mint, for this purpose. Perhaps a culinary knot planted at the gravelled entrance to a walled kitchen garden? It could be walked across to release scent with no permanent damage to the plants, although I accept its maintenance might be rather troublesome. I think it would be worth the effort to a passionate gardener and will include it in my list of 'gardens to make one day'. Other soft plants which would resent being trodden on include thrift, *Armeria maritima* and gillyflowers, which we call pinks or, less appropriately, carnations.

There are of course other plants which give interest to the winter knot garden. Clipping plants into ornamental shapes has been practised for thousands of years for practical purposes: increasing fruit production, creating shade and raising delicate fruit from the ground to prevent bruising. In the knot garden setting, topiary emphasises the formality of the style. It can create important punctuation marks within the informality of a fully planted knot, providing breathing space amongst the riotous collection of flowers and colour. Symmetrically placed topiary ensures the garden retains structure in the planting throughout all seasons and is the most important architectural effect achieved by soft landscaping. In a simple knot, topiary is most striking when planted as specimens within the compartments, mirrored and replicated throughout the design.

Spirals, lollipops, cones, tetrahedrons and a range of more exotic shapes from peacocks to squirrels can be made or bought. Plants can be trained from young cuttings, teasing the leader around an iron framework season after season until, eventually, a mature piece of topiary develops, or mature plants can be sculptured by cutting into the growth to make an ornamental shape. Mature topiary can be expensive and may occasionally prove unreliable in cold winters, especially if the plants are imported from the Mediterranean, but it does have instant impact in a garden.

Yew, box, holly and privet are traditional plants for clipping into ornamental shapes but many common shrubs can also be used, including photinia, euonymus and cotoneaster. These are hardy even in cold areas so can be relied upon for winter interest.

Winter flowering plants also have a place in the knot garden. The Christmas rose, *Helleborus niger*, is the earliest of the hellebores with flowers appearing from December to March. *Helleborus orientalis*, the Lenten rose, begins her season about February and should continue to flower until early April. With *H. foetidus* and *H. argutifolius* flowering from March until the end of April, this invaluable plant species should be invited into any winter garden.

**145. At Hatfield the lime tinged new shoots on the box hedge are a lovely backdrop to the acid green flowers of *Helleborus foetidus*.**

## SPRING

If hedges demanded our full attention in the winter, it is the turn of bulbs to steal the spring limelight. I am continually amazed at the miracle which takes place each year when the dry onion-like object planted in autumn produces a dramatic flower the following spring. I remember my astonishment at horticultural college when I dissected a narcissus bulb and saw the juvenile flower bud developing inside the scales of the dormant bulb. Even more wonderful is the speed with which *Anenome blanda* produces foliage and flowers after a small dry lump of unpromising tuber is pessimistically put in the ground in autumn. By early spring beautiful blue, white or pink flowers cheer even the dullest day and the weariest heart. Do take advantage of the mail order catalogues offered by specialist bulb suppliers as the delight these plants bring more than repays their initial cost.

Bulbs, rhizomes, tubers and corms are food storage organs which allow the plants to pass through periods of dormancy before they develop leaves, stems and finally flowers. Whether used as mass planting in the compartments of a parterre or as companion plants in the mixed display of a planted knot, flowering bulbs can provide colour and interest every month of the year. One of the most hysterical horticultural fashions which occurred early in the seventeenth century was associated with tulips when carriages and even houses were exchanged for recently introduced bulbs. Many of these were similar to the colourful parrot and viridiflora tulips available today and were particularly prized for their vibrant, colour-streaked petals, the ornamentation caused by a viral infection.

Using flamboyant tulips in the knot provides a wonderful opportunity to turn your nose up at the sophisticated gardening which occasionally ensnares us all. Outrageous flowers have no place in the serene white garden or the cool blue border, but given the foil of a green box hedge a parrot tulip will show off to its heart's content. There are about ten varieties listed in bulb catalogues but they vary in their degree of frilliness and the fussiest ones are the best. 'Flaming Parrot' is my favourite perhaps because I so rarely have the opportunity to work with yellow and red – especially on one flower! 'Black Parrot' always tempts me but has proven slightly unreliable, sometimes dark red at best and rarely being as deeply frilled as 'Flaming Parrot'. Try viridiflora tulips too with their green-streaked petals and, if you do hanker after sophistication, there are no classier tulips than the lily flowered varieties. 'White Triumphator' is serene in her beauty with a long, strong stem and elegant, waisted flowers. 'West Point' is a yellow form and 'Marilyn' has creamy white flowers with fine strawberry streaks. The small species tulips are delightful in their simplicity and would be horrified to share the spotlight with their brash relatives. However, planted *en masse* and left to naturalise, little *Tulipa chrysantha* and *T. clusiana* will steal your heart. Plant them in compartments near the edge of the knot where you can appreciate them. Tulips should be planted three times deeper than their own depth in well drained soil. If your soil is light and free draining you may be able to leave the bulbs in the soil, but otherwise lift them when the leaves have turned brown and store them in a dry place. Species tulips should naturalise in well drained soil.

Selecting narcissi is as subjective as choosing decorations for your home. There are big and bold daffodils, ones with pink or orange trumpets, doubles and singles, species or hybrids, but there is one rule which should be applied to choosing narcissi for your knot garden – make sure they have fine leaves. Large hybrids such as 'Carlton' make vibrant displays in large areas but are too hefty for the compartments of a knot. The leaves, which must be allowed to turn brown before they are tidied in any way, would swamp small plants and emerging shoots. My preference is for the small species narcissi. I adore *N. bulbocodium*, with the delightful hoop petticoat and think *N. cyclamineus* too sweet for words. *N. triandrus albus* is a lovely cream colour but perhaps my all time

favourite daffodil is the 'Pheasants Eye', *N. poeticus* with single white petals and a small yellow eye edged with deep red. Plant narcissi as tulips, but leave the bulbs undisturbed for several years.

Once late spring arrives another favourite selection of bulbs begin to flower. The fritillaries are a wide ranging group of plants, from the small but exquisite snakeshead, *Fritillaria meleagris*, to the ridiculous crown imperial. This is a large, smelly bulb which will arrive in autumn and should be planted immediately, laid on its side, 20 cm deep on a small bed of gravel or grit to improve drainage. The previ-

ous year's flower stem leaves a large hole in the top of the bulb which could fill with moisture and cause the bulb to rot, but planting it on its side should avoid this problem. *Fritillaria imperialis* 'Lutea' is golden yellow and *F. imperialis* 'Aurora' orange. Both smell vile but look wonderful, circling the holly spiral at the centre of the Museum knot and at this distance we do not smell them anyway. Expensive but exquisite is the most beautiful fritillary of all: *Fritillaria persica* with deep purple bells and smoky grey green leaves. Ask someone to buy a few bulbs as an early Christmas present.

**147. At Chenies Manor in Buckinghamshire bulbs are planted *en masse* in striking combinations like these magenta tulips with deep lilac violas.**

**146** *previous page*. **The Museum knot in spring featuring a favourite tulip, 'Flaming Parrot'.**

**148. Spring at Hatfield. A dramatic planting of euphorbia, hellebores, crown fritillaries and tulips set against the giant topiary crowns in the East Garden.**

Crocus, cyclamen and anemones are small and dainty and available in many different varieties. Snowdrops should be bought 'in the green' which means you buy them in late spring, after flowering and plant them as the foliage begins to die. They are unreliable when planted as dry bulbs as only a small percentage survive. One delightful hardy geranium, *Geranium tuberosum*, is grown from a tuber. The finely cut leaves emerge in early spring and purple flowers appear in April. The foliage then dies back completely when other hardy geraniums are just beginning to grow.

In a simple knot you may decide to use bulbs for seasonal displays. You could also include other plants such as pansies, wallflowers, forget-me-nots and stocks. Plant the bulbs first then, using a hand trowel, carefully plant the bedding in the compartments. You can have a lot of fun with colour schemes, changing

the theme annually and once the spring display has finished the plants can be removed and replaced with summer bedding, perhaps *Pelargoniums* or *Impatiens*.

Perhaps the hardest thing about choosing spring flowering bulbs is that catalogues arrive in August, in the heat of summer when the last thing you are thinking about is the following spring. By the time you naturally turn your thoughts to spring gardening, the best bulbs will have sold out. Try to order your bulbs early and your efforts will be repaid when you see them flower the following year.

**149. Spring bulbs at Chenies Manor, Buckinghamshire. The ruin is a romantic backdrop to the formality of the topiary and pleached trees.**

**151** *following page.* **Summer exuberance in the Museum knot with foxgloves and the shorter spires of** *Dictamnus albus* **'Purpureus'.**

**150. The newly restored Privy Garden at Hampton Court. The flowers favoured in William and Mary's time included familiar cottage annuals like cornflowers, opium poppies and marigolds.**

## HARDY ANNUALS AND BIENNIALS

Hardy annuals can be used to introduce informality to the planting. They differ both in habit and hardiness from the annual plants, such as petunia, lobelia and alyssum, you might use in hanging baskets or containers which are classed as tender annuals. All annuals live for only one season, germinating, growing, flowering and setting seed often within only a few months. Unlike the seed of tender annuals that of a hardy annual will survive outside through winter, remaining dormant in the soil until the warm spring sun encourages germination.

Some of the simplest plants are often the most effective in a knot garden and retain a charm reminiscent of the cottage garden. Many are indigenous and have been used in gardens for centuries. Hardy annuals can create a soft haze of colour, self seeding to produce flowering plants the following year. While this self seeding habit can be a nuisance, it is easily controlled by removing seed heads throughout summer or thinning out seedlings in spring.

*Calendula officinalis*, pot marigold, is a delight and has none of the stiffness of the similarly named French or African marigolds. I am always pleased to see the simple daisy-like flowers popping through other plants and am pleasantly surprised to find their bright orange petals cause no offence next to a pink rose or a red campion. Perhaps this is the essence of a cottage garden style; in the slightly chaotic disorder of informal planting everything seems to belong, colour co-ordinated or not.

A single packet of candytuft, *Iberis umbellata*, casually sprinkled in the garden several years ago continues to produce offspring in lovely shades of pink, lilac and white. As with many self sown plants, it puts itself into the most delightful places where you could never hope to introduce a plant yourself. Nestled snugly against the base of a rose, it forms quite a shrubby little plant and the haze of tiny flowers effectively hides the bare wood of the shrub rose. There are many flower heads on one plant and they all mature at different times, dropping seed throughout the season. In our mild garden some of the early seed germinates later in summer and the little plants manage to survive winter, tucked snugly behind the box hedge. The following year we are treated to a succession of flowers from May through to September, starting with the overwintered plants and ending with the ones which germinated that spring.

*Nigella damascena*, the romantically named love-in-a-mist, is a good value plant. Delicate, feathery leaves surround the prettiest blue flowers, each with a little, feathery crown. These last from June to August but yet more pleasure awaits; the seed head is a delicate, airy pod, topped by the same little crown and these last until the first frost cuts the plant down. I love *Nigella* in its simplest blue form but you can also buy seed for pink and white flowers as well as double forms.

These old fashioned plants have wonderful common names. *Delphinium consolida* is known as larkspur, which has such a happy sound, you immediately know this little plant will be a cheery addition to the garden. Larkspur seems to have little in common with the giant delphiniums of the herbaceous border, being even more delicate in habit than *Nigella*. Vivid blue flowers open from June to August and have the same irresistible habit of popping through other plants. Natural variations occur and you sometimes see lilac or pink forms.

Biennials have an extended life cycle of two years. They germinate and grow a basal rosette of leaves in the first year, overwinter and then produce a flower the following summer. The seed drops to the ground where it overwinters before germinating the following spring and the cycle begins again. You should introduce biennials to your garden for two consecutive years to ensure a future display every year. Occasionally biennials behave as perennials and instead of dying after flowering, the basal rosette of leaves continue to grow with offshoots developing at the side from which flower shoots eventually emerge. I prefer to remove the plant after flowering as the clump grows quite large when behaving as a perennial, taking too much space in the compartments.

The best known examples of biennials are foxgloves with their tall spires of lilac and pink bells. Pure white forms are available but the seed cannot be relied upon to remain pure. Bees find foxglove flowers irresistible and will cross pollinate plants and the stronger lilac species tends to dominate. Forms of mullein are also biennial and the best known is the majestic *Verbascum bombyciferum*. This can be rather dominating with branched flower stems reaching over a metre high, but if your knot garden is on a grand scale, mullein would be a dramatic contributor to the planting scheme.

Other biennials do not share the same rocket-like habit of foxglove and mullein although one uses the name. Sweet rocket, *Hesperis matronalis* is a delicate biennial with white, pink or lilac flowers which are heavily scented in the evening. Many old garden plants such as evening primrose, *Oenothera biennis* and honesty, *Lunaria biennis*, are, as their names suggest, biennials.

152. Hedges of *Lavandula officinalis*, box topiary and carpets of *Geranium macrorrhizum* and *Salvia* x *sylvestris* 'May Night' make this low maintenance parterre designed by Paul Miles elegantly effective.

## SUMMER PERENNIALS

Hardy perennials are plants you can generally rely on to flower each year without too much attention. The roots of perennials survive for many years but differ from shrubs because top growth never becomes woody but stays soft and green. Some perennials such as hellebores are evergreen, but most are deciduous and any part of the plant above the ground dies at the end of summer, leaving the hidden roots to survive in a dormant state until spring.

This is a wide and varied group of plants which provide a vast choice of colour, size and shape. Delicate pastels or hot vibrant colours can give breathtaking displays for much of the year. Some perennials are extremely vigorous, spreading rapidly and invasively from the rootstock, for example shasta daisy and golden rod, while others like peonies develop lax growth, collapsing heavily on to surrounding plants unless supported. Both categories are unsuitable for small knot gardens as the hedge could suffer from competition for moisture, nutrients and light and the physical damage caused by soft, heavy plants can be severe.

We rely on perennials in the garden for many months of the year but especially during summer. There are so many favourites it is difficult to single any out for special attention but perhaps *Tradescantia virginiana*, also known as *Tradescantia* x *andersoniana,* should be mentioned. Tradescantias in the Museum garden are a cross fertilised collection of blues, pinks, lilacs and whites. Their strap-like leaves surround a three-petalled flower with prominent golden stamen and they flower from June to September. They self seed quite vigorously and we never know what colour the flowers will be. If you are keen to colour co-ordinate your planting, buy named hybrids, but if you have several forms in the garden you will find seedlings are the result of cross fertilisation. The only way to guarantee colour is to divide an established clump.

There are several forms of campion and most are

**153. Broughton Castle, Oxfordshire. A lovely collection of summer flowering plants. Biennial foxgloves and sweet william mix with perennial *Lychnis coronaria*. Roses and alliums also play a critical part in this scene.**

suitable for the knot. It is difficult to refuse finding a place for *Lychnis coronaria* with its grey felty leaves and stems and magenta flowers from July to September. Although classed as short lived perennials, they self seed enthusiastically so you will never loose them. There is a pure white form which is rather lovely as well as one with white outer petals and a lilac centre. *Lychnis chalcedonica* is a quite different relative. It has sappy, bright green stems and leaves with small, cross shaped scarlet flowers in dense

heads. The flower shape accounts for the common name Maltese Cross.

Some perennials will flower a second time late in the summer if they are quite brutally cut down to the base once the first flowering has finished. Hardy geraniums are most reliable although some forms hardly stop flowering for long enough to cut. Nevertheless it is worth being ruthless as certain varieties can become loose and floppy later in the season but will form a tight clump of new leaves after cutting.

Amongst older forms are *G. sanguineum* or bloody cranesbill, a delicate plant with light pink flowers. The wonderfully aromatic *G. macrorrhizum*, has white, pink-flushed flowers while mourning widow, *Geranium phaeum*, has deep purple, sometimes almost black flowers. Our native herb robert, *Geranium robertianum*, deserves more appreciation than it is usually given and I enjoy seeing it self seeded around roses. It is naturally pink flowering but a lovely white form can be found. My recently discovered favourite hardy geranium is *G. pyrenaicum* with delicate lilac flowers or its white form, the magnificently named *G. pyrenaicum forma albiflorum*. These small flowers grow on long trailing stems so the plant can be grown behind roses or other perennials and the stems will weave through their neighbours so the little flowers seem to pop out of nowhere.

*Astrantia major*, a form of masterwort, is another perennial which can be cut back hard to encourage a second flowering. Parchment-like bracts surround tiny petals which form a pincushion head in the centre of the flower, coloured an unusual greenish pink. There are some lovely deep red forms but some of the finer hybrids can be expensive as they are not vigorous plants and true clones can only be had by division, not from sown seed.

I must include pinks, or gillyflowers. These delightful old plants have been used in gardens for centuries and continue to bring pleasure to those who know them. Modern carnations are a different breed, but it is the old fashioned pinks which have stolen my heart. Yet again we meet a promiscuous group of perennials and mention is made in historic gardening books of varieties with wonderful names such as 'Sops in wine' and 'Bat's double red'. These are still sold as named varieties and, although their promiscuity may cast some doubt on absolute authenticity, the flowers seem as close as I will ever need to the originals. Usually low growing plants, the tight mat of grey foliage is a perfect foil to the delicate pink, deep red or white petals. Pinks can be propagated quite easily from cuttings and you should take some

**154. Aquilegia at Hatfield.** Also known as columbine or Granny's bonnet, *Aquilegia vulgaris* has been grown in British gardens for centuries. It is invaluable for colour in early summer with a natural range including pink, lilac, purple and yellow. Named varieties can also be bought.

**155. Penstemon at Penrhyn Castle.** This lovely display mimics the character of carpet bedding, but uses the delicate habit of penstemon, a tender perennial, to great effect. The fuchsia are delightful too, but rest rather heavily on the box hedge.

each year as the original plants gradually become bare at the centre and will need replacing. There is a pink called *Dianthus carthusianorum* with a much taller habit and I first saw this growing in an enormous clump in the East Garden at Hatfield House many years ago. The leaves are quite green rather than grey, and the tiny magenta flowers grow on stems about 35 cm long. They are wonderful plants for the small knot, prolific flowerers, but taking up little space. Seek out the specialist suppliers of old fashioned pinks and if one of them can sell you *Dianthus* 'Elizabethan' you will be in their debt for ever.

Summer horticultural shows benefit from a vast array of specialist nurseries exhibiting and selling perennial plants. Try and visit shows, and order catalogues for the widest choice.

## SUMMER BULBS

Having already witnessed my enthusiasm for spring bulbs you may be surprised to see bulbs pop up again here, but the wide choice of summer flowering bulbs cannot go without mention. Summer bulbs also have the useful habit of flowering on strong upright stems which hold the flowers high above the hedge of the knot. This habit is ideal, especially when the bulbs are combined with softer, billowing perennials.

Once your name is registered with bulb suppliers they will not only send you their autumn selection in August, but in the grey days of January your spirit will lift at the arrival of their spring/summer catalogue. Unlike the difficulties of selecting spring bulbs in high summer, there is absolutely no problem in spending an evening in front of the fire, choosing summer bulbs for your new knot garden. You can select hardy bulbs which stay in the ground year after year, but you can also experiment with exotic, tender bulbs. These are more demanding and may need to be grown in a frost free greenhouse, before plunging the plant, pot and all, into the garden for a few weeks of glory. If this is too much work for you, stick with the hardy bulbs, but if you have the time and interest, you will be thrilled with the results of your labours.

Among the hardy bulbs are alliums and these are great favourites of mine. The popular large-headed varieties such as *A. aflatuense* and *A. giganteum* are fun but need to be used with care as they can be top heavy. I much prefer the smaller, oval heads of the drumstick allium, *A. sphaerocephalum*, which are deep magenta. They are reasonably priced which means you can plant a lot more drumsticks than big-heads for your money and I think the overall effect is better. I have much enjoyed getting to know *Allium bulgaricum* (syn. *Nectaroscordum siculum*) in recent years. It fascinates me because the lovely flowers

156. Iris at Rousham. Iris are effective in large groups, but only flower for a relatively short period. Soft plants such as hardy annuals or perennials can be planted as companions and will benefit from the vertical structure of the iris leaves.

**157. Agapanthus at Bodysgallen. Blue agapanthus is a delightful plant. Here the white form gives the planting a cool serene character. The leaves are quite large and will take up a lot of room in the compartments of a knot.**

**158** *following page*. **The Museum knot in June.** *Rosa gallica* **'Officinalis' only flowers for two weeks in June but it is a lovely rose with a heavy scent.**

hang down, but the seed pods turn up as they ripen. The flowers are a curious mixture of green, white and plum and are shaped like open bells.

I have never had any interest in growing the absurd gladioli you find in florists shops, but *Gladiolus byzantinus*, is altogether different. Delicate and unobtrusive, this little plant self seeds freely, sending offspring romping around the garden. The bell-like flowers are wine coloured so look good planted with old fashioned roses. Seedlings grow like fine blades of grass for a couple of years before the bulbs are large

enough to flower. Either leave them where they are or lift and pot them on, returning them to the garden in their second or third year.

Although I have never fallen wildly for the large iris varieties, I do think they have a place in the knot garden and historically they are important plants. We grow *Iris florentina* and *I. germanica* both of which are blue, as is *Iris foetidissima*. The flowers of this plant are less significant but in autumn large seed pods open to reveal masses of bright orange berries. You should know that the common name for this plant is stinking iris! If you are not planting an historic garden, you can choose from a vast selection. For mass displays in June, the group called Dutch iris are good and colours range from white, through pale lilac to deep purple as well as yellow.

The Garden at The Ark is the second garden owned by the Museum and planting is not tied to any historic period. Here we grow *Iris pallida* 'Argenteo-variegata'. Delicate blue flowers appear in June but the leaves provide year round interest. The grey green foliage has vertical cream variegations which look lovely, especially growing through the similarly coloured *Lamium maculatum* 'White Nancy'.

Eremurus are good fun but most appropriate for the large knot. The flower spike is over a metre high and contains hundreds of small flowers, but it is the size of the tuber which dictates its planting position. Several thick, long roots trail out from a central corm and these need to be laid flat in the soil so require a large planting hole. If you are lucky enough to garden on the scale of the East Garden at Hatfield House, foxtail lilies are worth a try.

Why does the beautiful but much hated lily beetle exist? Without it I would have no hesitation in planting lilies in profusion wherever I work, but having seen their devastating effect on these beautiful plants, I feel the burden of responsibility weighs too heavy. If you have never seen this beetle, start growing lilies and it will find its way to you. Stamping on what seem to be rather elegant relatives of the ladybird is the only effective way to be rid of the pest. The brown, gooey substance and the larvae it protects should also be removed and disposed of before your plants are stripped in the blink of an eye.

Now you have been warned, feel free to fall under the seductive spell of lilies. The easiest and most prolific in our light soil is the Turk's cap, *Lilium martagon*, with pink reflexed petals. It self seeds around the knot and seems quickly to develop flowering sized bulbs. The lovely white form is expensive. *Lilium longiflorum* is white and elegant and *L. speciosum rubrum* looks exotic and delicate although it is as hardy as any other. For something different, grow the difficult and shy, but lovely, *L. nepalense* which hangs its pale green head to hide the deep maroon interior to the flowers. I had a fine collection of these in pots at home until I carelessly went on holiday one year and left them as a feast for the lily beetle.

To extend interest into autumn, plant *Nerine bowdenii*, the Guernsey lily. It needs a warm spot in a mild location, so you may need to rely on growing the bulbs in pots if you live in a cold area. The flowers are clear pink in colour, which I find slightly disconcerting during early autumn; this colour seems more at home in mid summer planting schemes. Also unreliably hardy, less elegant but much more fun is *Eucomis autumnalis,* which looks like an exploding firework with its chunky spike of creamy white flowers topped by a tuft of green leaves.

Another late interest tuberous plant, also said to be half hardy, is *Mirabilis jalapa*, Marvel of Peru or four o'clock plant. Small, fragrant trumpets of red, yellow, pink or white flowers open late in the afternoon. This plants survives year after year in our mild garden, self seeding and becoming quite invasive at times. I do become rather complacent in recommending such plants as gardening in a mild location has lulled me into a false sense of security. However, I will let you into a secret. Although *Mirabilis* is a tuber, you can sow seeds in April and have a flowering plant by late August, so treat it as an annual.

If you are interested in growing other non-hardy bulbs, the small cannas are lovely. We have *Canna indica*, Indian shot, growing for period interest and it is a sweet plant, less vulgar than the cannas which so well suit Victorian park planting schemes. Some dahlias, such as the infamous 'Bishop of Llandaff' are delicate enough to grow in a knot garden, and the lovely *Ornithagalum arabicum* which has black, jewel-like seeds is delightful. Two other forms, *O. nutans* with green streaked petals and *O. thyrsoides,* or chincherinchee are also good. Finally, if you have a cool greenhouse, grow *Polianthes* 'The Pearl' to enjoy one of the heaviest scents of any garden plant.

## ROSES AND CLIMBERS

I mentioned earlier that the choice of narcissi is personal and subjective. This is an understatement compared to the passion dedicated to choosing roses. For my own part I should say that you are not going to find any hybrid tea or patio roses in this chapter, and only one floribunda, but that is my choice, not yours.

Roses supply an element of permanence to the internal planting of a knot as their woody framework persists for many years and although leaves fall in winter the structure of the plant remains. They are invaluable in historic gardens as specimens such as *Rosa gallica* 'Officinalis', the apothecary's rose, were used for medicinal purposes from medieval times. Old fashioned roses have a charm and elegance often missing from the disease resistant, continuous flowering hybrids of today.

The sense of smell is one of the most important to be stimulated in the garden and roses contribute a heady perfume of nostalgic familiarity. The intimate, enclosed setting of a knot garden is one which calls out for scented plants. Use rose catalogues to help you to draw up a shortlist based on colour, size, repeat or continuous flowering and scent. Availability is best during late summer and autumn when orders can be placed to reserve roses which will be despatched by mail as bare rooted stock throughout the dormant season.

Old roses fall into several groups which include those with romantic names like gallicas, centifolias and damasks. Some of the groups contain individual roses which repeat flower and it is from these I make my selection, including China roses, Portlands and Bourbons. Others will sneak in along the way as well as a couple of modern roses which have been bred in an old fashioned style. I do have a soft spot for a particular old rose group which only flowers once and this is the Alba roses. My fondness is due to the fact that individuals from this group have survived and even flourished in difficult growing conditions in the Museum garden. Albas seem to remain healthy and

vigorous in situations which make other groups curl up their toes and die. They may flower only once but *R.x alba*, the White Rose of York, *R. x alba* 'Maxima', the Jacobite rose and *Rosa x alba* 'Semi-plena' have all earned my respect.

This January I was surprised to notice flower buds on four different roses in my garden at home. One of them was 'Iceberg' which seems slightly out of character with the rest of the selection, but I always find myself saying 'good old Iceberg'. It is well known for flowering far into winter and usually has white flowers although these can sometimes be delicately tinged with pink. It is fragrant and reliable although weak strains sometimes find it hard to resist mildew in summer. 'Iceberg' is best pruned to a medium sized shrub, about 1.2 metres high and wide.

Another of my January rosebuds was on the romantically named 'Reine des Violettes'. This is a Victorian rose full of charm from earlier periods and is made up of a mass of petals in shades of lilac and purple and has a delicate scent. I visited a large rose nursery last summer and broke all my own rules by buying this plant on a hot August day, when it was in full flower and my garden was dry as a bone. This is strong recommendation indeed and reminds me that all gardeners should be impulsive now and again.

Who would be without 'Old Blush China', the 'monthly rose' and my third bud? As a China rose it needs lots of sun but little pruning. Loose clusters of pale pink, lightly scented flowers deepen in colour as they age. A modern rose of old fashioned style completed the set of four. 'Mary Rose' is a loose petalled, fragrant pink rose and forms a twiggy plant 1.2 metres high and wide. It is one of the few modern roses in my own garden where it earns its place.

My priorities in selecting my own roses are the ability to repeat or continuously flower and a good scent. Occasionally I have to demand a tolerance to shade, but I wonder if I am also guided by the degree of romance in a rose's name. 'Boule de Neige' is a Bourbon therefore almost guaranteed to be heavily scented, which it is. Full creamy white flowers appear

repeatedly through summer and it has very shiny, healthy leaves. 'Honorine de Brabant' is another romantically named Bourbon with pink flowers that have lovely maroon and crimson marks. The scent of this rose can only be described as 'fruity'. It is my substitute for *Rosa gallica* 'Officinalis' from which the better named 'Rosa Mundi' is a sport and is the very old, striped rose which sadly only flowers for two weeks in early summer and struggles in the far from ideal conditions of the Museum garden. My last Bourbon is 'Mme Pierre Oger' which has heavy, full cup-shaped flowers coloured pale pink and heavily perfumed. 'Mme Pierre Oger' flowers heavily all summer long.

Portland roses have been superseded to some extent by Bourbons but I grow 'Comte de Chambord' from this group and chose it because it only grows about a metre high and wide and has a good scent. The flowers are pink and open flat and full.

Two roses in the Museum garden repeat flower and it is a real pleasure to see them in July or August when all we have left otherwise is memories from June. One of these, *Rosa* 'de Rescht', is a Portland rose and it has lovely deep crimson flowers which appear across the top of the foliage. Unusually, the other is a damask and it is the oldest repeat flowering rose. 'Quatre Saisons', also known as the 'Rose of Four Seasons' or 'Autumn Damask', is scented and has a loose open habit with almost double, pale pink flowers.

It is only in recent years that I have come under the charm of roses, and I think this may be the result of spending years in suburban areas where sadly neglected hybrid teas were planted in regimented rows leading to a front door. Roses should be removed from such situations so they can do no more harm to vulnerable young minds. I hope you fall under the spell of old fashioned roses and again suggest that you spend your next summer visiting gardens which are famous for their collections. Try the walled garden at Mottisfont Abbey in Hampshire where the National Trust have their collection of old roses. There could be no better starting place.

Perhaps you were surprised to see climbers recommended as plants for a knot garden, but they play an important role in planting schemes, not only providing plant interest, but having structural impact as well. This is simply because they need a support to climb up or scramble through and whether this is made from delicate ironwork, elaborate timber or is simply a collection of twiggy hazel stems, impact is immediate and effective.

Many roses can grow up sturdy supports. These need not be ramblers or climbers, which could be too vigorous, but some of the large shrub roses are also suitable. A Bourbon, *Rosa* 'Bourbon Queen' is a good example. It has pink flowers, which are shaded darker towards the centre, flowers in mid June then repeats later in summer. 'Blush Noisette' is a lovely little rose, classed as a repeat flowering climber and said to reach 4 metres high but I have always found it less vigorous. It has many slender branches which can be tied in to make a dense network of spiralled wood around a timber or iron support. The flowers appear in small clusters, lilac pink in colour and the scent is lovely and reminiscent of cloves. 'New Dawn' is a modern rose which grows to about 2.5 metres tall. The blush pink, scented flowers repeat through summer. It is a very reliable, trouble free rose.

Annual climbers can be used to contribute colour throughout summer and are usually grown easily from seed. They can be used in combination with permanent climbing plants, especially roses which can be decorated with sweet peas or morning glory. *Mina lobata* is a vibrant climber with red and yellow claw-like flowers appearing *en masse* through late summer. It is tender and grown as an annual in Britain, but is very useful for late interest. Beans are decorative and useful and can be grown in either the vegetable parterre or an ornamental knot garden. The scarlet flowers of runner beans are very beautiful, but if you want something different try the hyacinth bean with vivid lilac flowers followed by deep purple pods.

Clematis can be effective, forming a flowering cascade from the top of a support. Less vigorous forms and late flowering species and cultivars which

159 *previous page*. **Roses tumbling and cascading at Broughton Castle, Oxfordshire. Roses are planted in the compartments but also used in borders around the knot enveloping the whole garden in colour and scent.**

160. **This strong yellow rose injects a lively note into the East Garden at Hatfield.**

require pruning back to 30 cm from the ground in spring are specially useful. An irresistible choice is *C. viticella* 'Purpurea Plena Elegans' with *C. v.* 'Etoille Violette' coming a close second. We grow both in The Garden at The Ark; the former, less vigorous one, grows up a vertical post and the other is tied into the roof of a small arbour. If you fancy a challenge, there is a lovely, but difficult clematis called *C. florida* 'Sieboldii' which has a sparse, delicate habit. The flowers are white with prominent purple stamens. It would be lovely tied into a delicate iron support, but it needs a sunny, sheltered position.

## HERBS AND THE POTAGER

The association of knot gardens with herbs is appropriate. Herbs can be traced back to the earliest gardens and are well documented in monastery and physic gardens. They are a wide ranging group; any plant with medicinal, culinary or aromatic use can be classed as a herb but we usually think of scented, woody plants originating in the Mediterranean, for example, lavender and thyme. Herbs can be quite demanding as they are often vigorous plants. You will need primed secateurs always to hand so that lax or invasive plants can be clipped and prevented from swamping neighbours or the hedge. Chosen carefully, however, herbs can be a great addition to the knot garden, either as companions to other plants or as mass planting as demonstrated in the striking examples at Ham House (title-page and plate 144).

Herbs contribute colour and textural interest from both flowers and foliage and often release strong scent, especially in hot sunshine, and their cu-

linary and medicinal potential offers a further dimension to the garden. There are many herbs suitable for the knot and it is fascinating to research which meet all your requirements – ornamental, culinary, medicinal, aromatic etc. Be sure you understand the habit of growth before you introduce a herb to the knot as some can be difficult to eradicate if they prove invasive. Woodruff and balm can both become a nuisance in the wrong place and it may take several seasons to completely remove them.

One of the herbs I value as an ornamental plant is *Allium schoenoprasum*, or chives. I have an enormous crop in the vegetable garden and my young daughter learnt from an early age that these were the only plants she was allowed to pick and eat. The lilac pompon flowers also taste delicious and can be used to brighten up a salad or for sprinkling on new potatoes. These cheerful flowers bob around on delicate stalks in the slightest breeze.

Fennel and dill are both lovely for their bright green, feathery foliage. Bronze fennel, *Foeniculum*

**162. Lavender at Boscobel. A good way to use herbs is to fill compartments with a single species.**

**161 and 163 *right*. Vegetables can offer the same creative opportunities as seasonal bedding. In Katherine Swift's garden coloured lettuce leaves are as effective as flowers. 'Cut and come' crops allow the display to be kept going over a long period as only a few leaves at a time are taken from the plants.**

*vulgare* 'Purpureum' has bronze tinged leaves which are especially lovely when young. The delicate umbrella flowers appear in summer and the seed heads which follow are admittedly generous in their distribution. The trick with all the vigorous self seeding plants is to be ruthless in spring when the seed germinates and pull out everything you do not want. Dill, *Anethum graveolens*, is shorter than fennel but similar in all other ways, being light and feathery in the foliage and carrying yellow umbelliferous flowers in summer. In my vegetable garden last year I grew fennel and dill with large sunflowers. These had a backdrop of hazel hurdles supporting climbing orange nasturtiums and the picture was completed by the rosemary hedge which forms the edge to the whole garden. I was delighted.

# DESIGNING YOUR KNOT

Now is the time to sit down with paper and pencil and begin work on a design. There are plenty of stimulating images here to inspire you and remember that the origins for many historic designs were found in other arts such as embroidery, metalwork, joinery and glazing. Look around your home and see if you find any architectural features which could form the beginnings of a knot design. Jewellery, fabric, wall paper and a host of other day to day objects may have patterns which can be adapted. Celtic designs with powerful weaving images particularly appeal to me and seem especially appropriate for knot gardens.

I hope your enthusiasm to begin the design is not dampened when you turn the next few pages as the exercises might remind you of school geometry or technical drawing classes. But I am sure that by working through them you will gain the confidence to begin your own design. We start with a simple pattern drawn with a pencil, ruler and compass, then develop it into a knot garden design by widening the single lines to represent a hedge and drawing to scale. The last point is very important; drawing to scale is the only way to ensure your design will fit into the space you have for your garden.

The exercises all use metric measurements which may cause concern to some. Having grown up using feet and inches, I reluctantly made the transition to metres and centimetres when I began work as a garden designer. The process can be slow and painful but is really worth the effort as measurements based on units of 10 rather than 12 are much easier to calculate. However, those who prefer to use imperial measurements will find conversion tables on page 146.

I always draw in pencil on tracing paper fixed to a sheet of graph paper. This system enables me to use the grid of the graph paper, based on 1 cm squares, for guidance and means mistakes and alterations can be erased easily. The following exercises use A4 paper, but you may need bigger sheets if you are designing a large garden. The other basic equipment you will need is as follows: *pencil, rubber, scale ruler, compass, 360 degree protractor.*

The Italian architect Alberti published his theories of symmetry in *De Re Aedificatoria* in the mid fifteenth century and many of the same principles still apply to formal design. Traditionally knots were symmetrical, contained within a square, with triangles, circles, semicircles and internal squares used to make geometric patterns. It is immensely satisfying to create these shapes with compass, ruler and pencil and the simple diagram in the first exercise will introduce you to using the equipment and developing patterns.

**Exercise 1**

*Lay your A4 tracing paper over the graph paper and secure with tape.*

*Using a hard pencil and a ruler, draw a square with sides measuring 10 cm.*

*Draw the diagonal lines **ab** and **cd** in light pencil as shown in the diagram. These are guide lines only, not part of the overall design.*

*Attach your pencil to the compass, positioning the compass point at the centre of the square where the two diagonal lines cross. Open the compass until the pencil just touches the square at **f**.*

*Lock the compass, then draw a circle which should fit neatly inside the square.*

*Retain the compass setting and position the point at **c**. Draw the arc **ef**.*

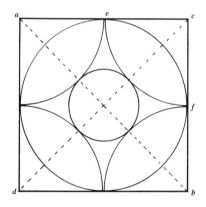

*Repeat this at each corner.*

*Finally, place the compass point at the centre once more, but reposition the setting so you draw a circle which fits snugly inside the arcs at the centre of the pattern.*

On completing Exercise 1 you will have drawn an attractive pattern but a little more work is needed for a knot garden design. In the first exercise you drew a square with sides measuring 10 cm, but this time you will be using a scale of 1:100 to draw a garden with sides of 10 metres. Your drawn square will be the same size as the last one but this time think of it as a garden measuring 10 metres square.

A knot garden hedge is approximately 30 cm wide and a design drawn at scale 1:100 should incorporate mirrored lines 3 mm smaller than the originals to represent the mature hedge, demonstrating that your design will be as effective in the garden as it is on paper. In intricate patterns the single lines can leave tiny compartments which would be totally filled by the mature hedge, and this method of using mirrored lines shows such detail clearly.

**The petal**

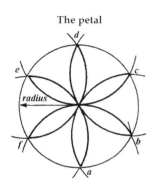

## Exercise 2

This takes you through the process of designing a knot garden step by step.

*Familiarise yourself with the scale 1:100 where 1 cm on paper equates to 1 metre on the ground.*

*Using tracing paper fixed to graph paper, draw a square to represent a garden measuring 10 metres on each side.*

*Draw the diagonal lines as faintly as you can.*

*Draw a second square with sides measuring 9.4 cm centrally inside the original square as shown on the diagram.*

*Position the compass point at the centre of the square. Fix the radius to draw a circle which fits inside the inner square.*

*Reduce the compass measurement by 3 mm and draw an inner circle.*

*Retaining this setting, position the compass point at each corner of the inner square and draw an arc.*

*Re-set the compass to the same radius as the larger circle*

**An octagon in a square**

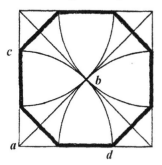

**An octagon in a circle**

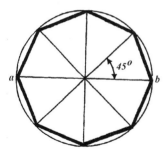

*and repeat the arcing exercise from the same corner points.*

*Draw the small central circle with a mirrored line 3 mm smaller.*

*Rub out any lines which interfere with the pattern; i.e., where arcs meet the outer circle.*

Notice how different hedge materials can be denoted simply by deciding which lines should continue and which are to be erased. Repeat the design several times, each time changing the crossovers and overlapping lines. Imagine where one species would end and another should be introduced.

Try the second exercise again, this time using A3 sized paper and a scale of 1:50. This is the most comfortable scale to work in and it is especially useful for planting plans. Be aware that 1 metre on the ground equates to 2 cm on paper and the hedge thickness will now be 6 mm. If you have a tiny garden or find it difficult to work in small detail, a scale of 1:20 could be used.

The following shapes can all be drawn easily with a pencil, compass and protractor and you may find them useful when you work on your own design.

### The petal

*Draw a circle.*

*Retaining the same compass setting, place the point of your compass at **a** and draw arc **fb**.*

*Continue around the circle, repeating this pattern by placing the compass point where the arcs touch the edge of the circle.*

### An octagon in a square

*Draw a square using graph paper as a guide.*

*Lightly draw the two diagonals to position the centre **b**.*

*Place your compass point at **a** and set it to width **ab**.*

*Draw arc **cd**.*

*Repeat for the other three corners.*

*Draw in the shape of the octagon by joining the points where the arcs touch the square*

### An octagon in a circle

*Draw a circle.*

*Lightly draw the central horizontal line **ab** using the graph paper grid as a guide.*

*Place the central line of a 360 degree protractor over the line **ab**, then mark each 45 degree point.*

*Draw lines through the centre of the circle to join the 45 degree marks.*

*The angles of your octagon are where these lines cross the circle. Draw in the outline of the octagon.*

### A six pointed star

*Draw a circle.*

*Retain the compass setting and place the point at **a** which can be anywhere on the circumference of the circle.*

*Draw an arc from the centre to where the pencil touches the edge of the circle, point **b**.*

*Continue around the circle, placing the point at **b** to establish **c** and so on.*

*Join up the points of the star as shown on the diagram.*

### A square in a circle

*Draw a circle.*

*Lightly draw lines **ac** and **bd** using a protractor or the graph paper grid as a guide.*

*Join up the marks.*

Learning to draw geometric shapes is the best introduction to knot garden design and the discipline emphasises the importance of pattern, symmetry and shape. However, designs can also be drawn freehand and some of the images in Thomas Hill's *Gardeners Labyrinth* are clearly drawn without the use of technical equipment. With a little skill and imagination dramatic patterns can be made, some of which would be impossible to construct using drawing tools. You should continue to use tracing paper laid over graph paper to ensure the design is drawn to scale and to assist in symmetry and balance. Freehand patterns tend to evolve with an almost organic freedom which results in a design which can be quite different from the one you began. I find this an exciting and totally absorbing way to design knot patterns.

I worked on the freehand design shown here one evening and after two or three hours had a pattern I liked. I would plant the hedge marked **A** with dwarf box, **B** with cotton lavender to bring in a grey leaved contrast and use the bottle green of germander, *Teucrium chamaedrys*, for **C**. The design could be successfully adapted to incorporate water by widening **B** and making a rill.

### Exercise 3: Blake's 'True Lovers Knott'

Some designs need a combination of geometry with freehand drawing to develop the pattern. Images in the first part of the book are irresistible and if you decide to use one as a basis for your own design, you need to transpose it into a scale drawing. Exercise 3 is lengthy and complicated, but if you work through each stage carefully, using both freehand and geometry, you will find the pattern eventually builds up. The image I have used is Blake's **'True Lovers Knott'** (plate 2) which was also the inspiration for Rosemary Verey's knot at Barnsley House (plate 140). Blake's notes tell us the original garden was to be 32 feet square which converts to 9.75 metres, but we will once more draw a garden measuring 10 metres square, at scale 1:100.

### Diagram 1

*Draw a garden measuring 10 metres square, using scale 1:100.*

*Draw in diagonals **ab** and **cd**, then horizontal line **ef** and vertical line **gh**. With a compass, draw a quarter segment of a 1 metre (1 cm) circle at each corner and a half circle at points **e**, **f**, **g**, and **h**.*

*By measuring the reproduced image of Blake's knot, I calculate the inner lines of the large circle cross the diagonal line one quarter of its distance from the corner. Our diagonal lines measure 14 cm and a quarter of this measurement is 3.5 cm.*

*Set your compass to 3.5 cm, position the point at the centre where the diagonal lines cross, and draw a circle.*

*Enlarge the compass measurement by 3 mm, and draw a larger mirrored circle.*

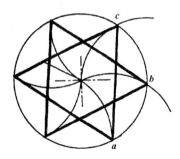

A six pointed star

A square in a circle

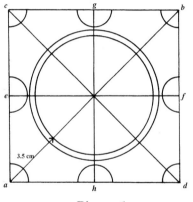

A freehand design

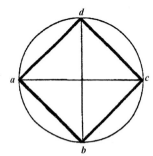

Diagram 1

**Diagram 2**

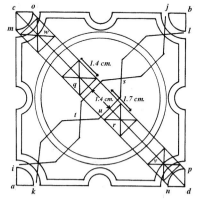

**Diagram 3**

**Diagram 4**

**Diagram 5**

You now have a geometric grid to help you develop the pattern. At the end of each section you need to attach another piece of tracing paper over the one you have just worked on. This will allow you to trace over lines you need whilst those which are part of the construction grid show through from earlier work without complicating the current drawing.

## Diagram 2

*Attach a second piece of tracing paper over the first.*

*Develop the mirrored lines around the perimeter of the design as shown in the diagram. The semicircles at e, f, g and h should have mirrored lines 3 mm smaller than the originals. At the corners, draw a quarter circle 3 mm larger than the originals, then another 3 mm larger again. The dotted lines indicate sections of the outline shape which should not be traced from the original.*

*Draw lines ij, kl, mn and op running parallel to the original lines. These are the guide lines for the weaving strands.*

## Diagram 3

This section includes some detailed measurements, taking guidance from the reproduced image as before. In this diagram I have used the diagonal line **cd** to show how the drawing is developed and diagonal **ab** demonstrates the outcome after this section has been worked through.

*Attach a third sheet of tracing paper to your work.*

*The weaving strands cross over at a halfway point between the centre of the design and the inner line of the circle; points q, r, s, and t. Mark in the positions on your drawing, 1.7 cm from the centre.*

*Notice that a square has been made in the centre of the drawing, labelled u on the diagram. Its sides measure 1.4 cm and you now need to reproduce the shape at q, r, s and t, taking these points as the centre of the squares.*

*Draw in the diagonal lines as shown at q and r.*

*Now draw identical squares at each corner, as shown at v and w.*

*Using these squares as a guide, develop the crossovers by erasing any lines which are no longer required. Your diagonals should now look like ab on the diagram.*

## Diagram 4

*Lay a fourth sheet of tracing paper over your work and prepare to draw in freehand.*

*I have shown the diagonal crossovers you constructed in the last exercise as dotted lines. Notice that these run along the centre of the double lines of the twisting threads.*

*Using Blake's image to guide you, begin by improving the shape of e, f, g and h. The diagram shows points e and g in their original form and f and h after they have been adapted. Notice how my hand drawn lines merge with compass and ruler lines.*

*Now develop the diagonal crossovers, remembering your guide lines run through the centre of the double lines of the twisting thread. Work in freehand.*

## Diagram 5

*Lay your fifth and final sheet of tracing paper over your work.*

*Now perfect the image, ignoring any construction lines which do not form part of the final design. Pay particular attention to which threads run under and which pass over one another. You may also need to improve the shape of the diagonal threads by making the loops a rounder shape.*

Congratulations if you manage to get to the end of Exercise 3. It is a challenge which either appeals to you or frustrates you, but the technique is useful if you want to transpose other designs. Remember how important it is to construct a geometric grid to help you draw the design. The same network of pencil lines would be repeated as string lines in the garden where you would follow the same steps to make the knot outside.

# THE PLANTING PLAN

Look at the drawing of your knot and think of it as a garden skeleton. Good structure ensures the success of any garden through the naked winter months when little decorative planting survives. In the knot garden, hedges provide this skeleton. A human face which benefits from good bone structure needs little additional decoration and an intricate cutwork parterre might remain similarly unadorned. Such simplicity can be effective and is perhaps one of the less appreciated facets of garden design. When visiting great gardens it is often refreshing to stumble across an area of simplicity and calm, away from the riotous colour and flamboyance of the herbaceous borders.

Historical sources demonstrate how planting styles developed as ornamental plants were introduced. Originally simple and unplanted, knots were later used to display newly introduced treasures within compartments; the hedges served as picture frames to exaggerate the beauty and importance of new discoveries. As plant hunters brought new plants to the country, so the knot garden became more heavily planted, as demonstrated in the gardens at Hatfield House and the Museum of Garden History. Documents such as the plant lists prepared for Hatfield House by John Tradescant the Elder, head gardener from 1610 to 1614, are invaluable. They contain information about plant introductions which enable gardens such as the knot at Tudor House in Southampton to be planted authentically for a specific period. If you are making an historic garden several books are available which give detailed information about period plants. A number of historic books have been republished with Gerard's *Herball* and Curtis's *Flower Garden Displayed* among the most valuable for information about early plants. Historic

or replica gardens like ours often sell their own plant lists and the Garden History Society can point you in the right direction. Many large cities have botanic or physic gardens full of plant material and information.

As our interest in gardening increases, it seems our enthusiasm to collect plants also accelerates. This can often be to great effect but a hazard is that the garden becomes overcomplicated and some plants are inevitably lost, unable to compete with the vigour of energetic neighbours. It is useful to prepare a planting plan for any new garden, ensuring plants have sufficient room to develop and thrive. In the confined planting areas of a knot, this is perhaps particularly important. Some people find the discipline of a planting plan restrictive and prefer to work in the equivalent of a freehand style. This is certainly exciting and challenging for the experienced designer but those new to the art of planting design can find the security of a plan gives confidence to their work. A planting plan can be complex, detailing every part of the garden, or it can be simple, showing only the crucial permanent plants such as roses, shrubs and key herbaceous specimens. It is often pleasing to allow some areas to develop in a more natural way, introducing an impulsive informality to frolic amongst the composed order of hedges, shrub roses and topiary.

A professional designer uses a metric circle template to design planting plans and these are available at good stationers. 1:50 is a comfortable scale for planting plans and if the garden design has been drawn to the same scale another sheet of tracing paper can be laid over the original plan, which you can then work on. If preferred, a plan can be drawn freehand using the graph paper as a guide and it is often as well to combine both methods, freehand being useful for tiny plants such as creeping herbs. Planting plans ensure that each plant is specifically chosen for its size, shape, colour, habit, texture, etc., and is properly positioned with sufficient room to grow. Specimen plants such as roses and large herbaceous can be planted individually, but smaller plants are more effective in groups of odd numbers. To simplify the drawing and speed up the design process, plants can be grouped into approximate sizes, rather than drawing individual varieties to a specific size. Hedge plants can be shown as a continuous symbol with a small cross detailing individual plant positions. Bulbs can be indicated with small crosses throughout the area but this can make the graphics rather confusing. It is preferable simply to indicate how many of a certain variety are planted within a compartment.

On the left is a guide to groups and template circle numbers drawn at 1:50.

A planting plan for the Museum knot garden

**Plant Template Guide**

**Shrub roses** (1m). Template 20 = 2cm

**Large herbaceous**,

    e.g., *Euphorbia wulfennii* (60cm).

    Template 12 = 1.2cm

**Medium herbaceous**,

    e.g., *Penstemon* 'Garnet' (45 cm).

    Template 9 = 0.9cm

**Small herbaceous**,

    e.g., *Alchemilla mollis* (30cm).

    Template 6 = 0.6cm

The next diagram is of the Museum knot with key plants detailed. We still have the original plant lists dating back to 1976 when the garden was first made, together with a key to locate specific plants within the design. This was a great help to me when I first began working in the garden because although some plants had died or had been moved, many could still be identified from the list; a great comfort to a new gardener. It is important to mention here that planting plans are set in soil, not stone and it is unreasonable to expect a garden to remain unchanged over many years. Plants may die or become too big for their original positions, and it is also refreshing to redesign areas to introduce new interest.

There are many more plants growing in the knot but the plan shows key and special interest specimens. The remaining herbaceous perennials could be drawn on the plan or listed, for example; 'around each *Rosa* 'de Meaux', 3 No. *Tradescantia virginiana* and 3 No. *Thymus officinalis*'.

| | |
|---|---|
| + | 480 No. *Buxus sempervirens* 'Suffruticosa' |
| o | 72 No. *Santolina chamaecyparissus* |
| A | 1 No. *Ilex altaclarensis* 'Golden King' (spiral) |
| B | 1 No. *Rosa gallica* 'Versicolor'   x 4 |
| C | 1 No. *Rosa burgundica*   x 2 |
| D | 1 No. *Rosa* 'de Rescht'   x 2 |
| E | 1 No. *Rosa gallica* 'Versicolor'   x 4 |
| F | 1 No. *Rosa gallica* 'Officinalis'   x 4 |
| G | 1 No. *Rosa* 'de Meaux'   x 4 |
| a | 5 No. *Fritillaria imperialis* 'Aurora' with 5 No. *Lilium candidum*   x 2 |
| ai | 5 No. *Fritillaria imperialis* 'Lutea' with 5 No. *Lilium candidum*   x 2 |
| b | 7 No. *Sternbergia lutea* |
| c | 1 No. *Stachys officinalis* with 1 No. *Lathyrus vernus* 'Albo-roseus' |
| d | 5 No. *Fritillaria meleagris* 'Albus' with 5 No. *Erythronium dens-canis* |
| e | 3 No. *Armeria maritima* |
| f | 5 No. *Primula auricula* |
| g | 5 No. *Bellis perennis* |
| h | 3 No. *Fragaria moschata* |
| i | 3 No. *Origanum vulgare* 'Aureum' |

Here is a much simpler planting plan for an unplanted knot, using the design for Blake's 'True Lovers Knott' on which we have already worked. Individual hedge plants are detailed as well as recommendations for season bulb planting in the internal compartments. When you draw hedge symbols, you may find a variance in the number of plants you need in identical sections, so take an average but add a few extra plants to your order as a safeguard. Any plants left over after planting can be your stock for replacement and propagation.

+     130 No. *Buxus sempervirens* 'Suffruticosa'   x 2

o     130 No. *Teucrium chamaedrys*   x 2

*     8 No. *Santolina virens*   x 4

**A**     Light grey gravel laid over landscape fabric

**B**     50 No. *Tulipa* 'West Point' with
       50 No. *Cheiranthus* 'White Dame'   x 4

**C**     30 No. *Tulipa* 'Spring Green' with pansy
       'Clear Sky Primrose'   x 8

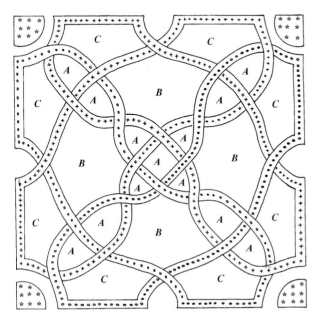

Planting plan for a simple knot

## METRIC CONVERSIONS

*If you work in imperial measurements, you will find the following information useful for the drawing exercise as well as for the surveying and setting out stages.*

1 metre equates to 1.0940 yards, so for the drawing exercise you could simply substitute a metre for a yard.

1 centimetre equates to 0.3937 inches.

30 cm can generally be taken as a rough substitute for 12 inches or one foot, although the calculation actually works out to 11. 81 inches.

If you buy graph paper with an imperial grid, you can work to scale using feet and inches:

˘ scale is very close to the metric 1:50, converting to 1:48 exactly. The planting plan exercise can be drawn in this scale where ˘ inch represents 1 foot, and 1 inch represents 4 feet.

1/8 scale is very close to the metric 1:100, converting to 1.96 exactly. My exercises at 1:100 can be drawn in this scale where 1/8 inch represents 1 foot, and 1 inch represents 8 feet.

# PREPARING THE GROUND

It is always exciting to watch a garden develop from a design which may have taken days or weeks to evolve. Eagerness to begin work is understandable, but wise gardeners ignore any temptation to rush into premature planting, and put their effort into thorough ground preparation instead. Compared with buying plants, the expense of importing manure may seem unglamorous and the physical effort demanded from soil cultivation can be unappealing, but it is worth remembering that any effort and expense contributed at this stage will be repaid time and again as the garden matures. Rarely is there another opportunity to improve the soil as efficiently as when it is completely bare. This is particularly so in the knot garden where hedges contribute permanent structure and should not be disturbed in maturity.

A gardener should be able to identify his soil type so that he can be aware of its strengths and weaknesses. There are a few basic categories which are easily identified although garden soils may fall midway between groups and incorporate characteristics from two or more types. It is undeniably hard work and can be expensive to improve soils, especially those at the extreme of the different types, but I am quite evangelical on this subject and always insist on soil improvement being treated as a priority.

The soil at the Museum is particularly poor, thin and free draining. It holds little moisture and nutrients and is really unsuitable for the old roses which are grown for the specific period interest. When any plant is grown in less than ideal conditions, it will not be as vigorous as usual and could also be vulnerable to pests and diseases. We continually feed, mulch and to some extent irrigate our roses but sometimes it feels like a losing battle. My recommendation is always to identify your soil type, improve it as much as you can with organic matter and fertilisers then plant, wherever possible, to suit your conditions. The historic theme of the Museum garden prevents us from always following this last piece of advice, but we are in an exceptional situation.

Clay soil is well known and easily identified, being like Plasticine in wet weather but baking to a hard, concrete material in summer. Whilst undeniably hard work, clay soils repay the gardener by being rich in nutrients. To transform an inhospitable clay soil into a rich loam, large amounts of organic matter are needed and in severe cases the addition of copious amounts of grit or pea shingle may be necessary to open air pockets and improve aeration. Where clay soil prevents free drainage of excess water, land drains may have to be installed. Lime in the form of calcium carbonate can be added as this helps to bind clay particles into the crumb-like structure needed to form a workable loam.

At the other end of the spectrum is sandy soil. Gritty to the touch, light and easy to work, this soil is very free draining. Moisture and nutrients are quickly lost and sandy soil is known as 'hungry and thirsty'. Improvement depends on making gritty particles bind together. Clay can be added in a process called marling, but heavy, sticky, well rotted farmyard manure is more easily available and effective in large amounts. The stickier the better.

Silty soil falls somewhere between clay and sandy soils, and can be identified by its smooth, silky texture. It tends to bind more easily than sandy soil and whilst it can compact under pressure it is generally much lighter than a clay soil. Silty soil retains moisture and nutrients reasonably well.

Chalky soil has only a thin layer of topsoil below which is the white chalk of the bedrock, clearly seen during cultivation. These soils can create the most difficult growing conditions, not only because of the thin topsoil but also because the chalk causes a high lime content in the soil. Some plants will not thrive, eventually developing yellow leaves from the effects of lime-induced chlorosis. Chalky soils can be improved by adding sufficient organic matter to raise the topsoil level, incorporating bulk and improving nutrient and water holding capacity. If plants do begin to deteriorate and show signs of chlorosis, a liquid treatment of sequestered iron may be necessary. Often it is appropriate to choose plants tolerant of the conditions, perhaps planting hedges with herbs like rosemary which tolerate poor, shallow soil.

Apart from structure there is another important element in ascertaining soil type. This is the pH measurement, or whether the soil is acid, neutral or alkaline, and it determines which plants grow healthily. For example acid loving plants such as azaleas and rhododendrons generally fail to thrive on alkaline soil, eventually deteriorating from the effects of chlorosis. While it is possible to take some steps to change the pH of a soil, these are often short term, expensive and to some extent futile. It is better to accept what you have and plant accordingly. Soil testing kits are available and the scale ranges from 1, extremely acidic, to 14, severely alkaline. Most soils fall between bands 4 and 8 with pH 6 to 7.5 being ideal for growing a wide range of plants.

Having identified your soil, you need to start thinking about preparing the ground where the knot is to be made. Various factors could influence its position in the garden, such as focal points from the house, but where possible choose level ground or an area which can be made level without too much work and expense. Small gradients can usually be corrected during the cultivation process when digging and raking moves the soil around. Steeper gradients might also be levelled at this stage but large piles of earth can build up during the work. Small, raised beds built from timber, brick or hurdles could be made to retain this excess soil on the highest side of the garden, allowing the remaining area to be levelled.

If the site slopes steeply, it may be necessary to employ professionals to terrace the land, working to the same principle as the raised beds detailed above, but on a much larger scale. Earth moving machinery could be brought in to move soil around but this operation should be carefully supervised to ensure valuable topsoil is removed and stored before levelling begins. When such heavy machines have been working in a garden, the earth can be badly compacted and the levelled subsoil should be deeply rotated and enriched with manure or compost. Gentle firming, preferably carried out by treading rather than machinery, should then take place before the topsoil is returned to the site.

Such work would be undeniably expensive as large walls or banks would also have to be built to hold the enormous amounts of soil excavated during the transformation from a sloping site to one with terraces. However, as the Victorians well knew, a large terrace is the perfect place for a parterre, as any elevated view emphasises the detail of design and pattern.

Once a level site is found or made the soil must be thoroughly cultivated. Cultivation really means digging, either by hand or using a rotovator and is inevitably hard work, especially on heavy clay soils. Large sites will probably need big machinery such as mechanical diggers and professional rather than domestic sized rotovators. Such machinery can be hired with or without operator, but if you are inexperienced, it is better to hand the responsibility to a professional. There is always the risk of unearthing cables or puncturing drains when using machines and liability and cost of repair would be yours if you are in charge of the equipment.

The first step in cultivating the soil is to remove weeds and turf by either physical or chemical methods. Chemicals should be used carefully, following manufacturers instructions about dilution and repeat applications and qualified professionals can be called in to carry out this work safely and effectively. This may be necessary if vigorous perennial weeds such as Japanese knotweed or ground elder are long established. Weeds and turf can be physically removed by digging, although care must be taken to ensure the full length of a tap root is extracted. Turf can be skimmed from the soil, cleaned of all perennial weeds and set to one side to be used as organic matter at subsoil level during double digging.

Digging breaks up compacted soils, improves drainage and increases the amount of oxygen available to roots. Single digging works the top layer of the soil to the depth of the spade blade, usually 25 cm, and is acceptable on light or previously well cultivated soils. Heavier soils, however, can develop a layer, or pan, of hard earth beneath the topsoil which roots may find impossible to penetrate and so be unable to search for moisture deep in the ground. The resulting shallow rooted plants are likely to die in periods of severe drought. Double digging involves the removal of the top layer or 'spit' of soil, allowing cultivation of the lower layer or subsoil. By digging and incorporating organic matter and nutrients at this stage, a much improved growing environment will be created. Turves can be laid, grass side down, at this subsoil level to create a layer of rich, organic material. Double digging is carried out in trenches and as one strip of subsoil is improved, topsoil from the next is turned into the trench, forked over and organic matter and nutrients are added.

Armchair gardeners may wrinkle their noses at the mention of manure but those with more experience know there is no fear of unpleasant smells from manure used in the garden. Strong smells of ammonia or other doubtful scents suggest the manure is not well rotted and too fresh for garden use where it would cause more harm than good. A manure heap which has been standing for a year or more has a warm, sweet fragrance and will enrich the soil in many ways. Manure is only one form of organic matter. Garden compost, seaweed and spent mushroom compost are others. Non-gardening friends look at me strangely when I enthuse about the rich fragrance of moist, warm mushroom compost on a cold autumn day. The smell alone tells you that goodness is going into the soil. Other products, such as hops, are available as waste material from industry, but some might contain residual chemicals which organic gardeners may prefer to avoid. There are also proprietary products on the market but these can be terribly expensive, prohibitively so when large amounts are required. Only generous applications of organic matter are truly effective and it is better to delay planting if a limited budget threatens such extravagance.

Organic matter introduces humus – a rich, dark, moist material which improves the soil in many ways. The stickiness of the organic material binds soil particles and creates the ideal crumb-like structure needed to retain moisture and create air pockets, ensuring oxygen is available to roots. The resulting open texture of the soil also provides an ideal environment for earthworms, which move easily around the cultivated earth, continually improving its condition. Organic matter also adds bulk to the soil and assists in the warming process in spring to ensure plant growth begins early in the season. As well as being incorporated during cultivation, organic matter should be added to the soil in a thick layer, no less than 12 cm deep, each spring to retain winter moisture and suppress weeds. Worms will pull the material down through the soil, constantly adding additional humus to the lower layers. The following spring there will be little sign of mulch on the surface, but the process should be repeated to ensure continual soil improvement.

After the soil has been cultivated existing levels have been disturbed and large air pockets remain beneath the surface. Left to its own devices the soil would settle unevenly, so the ground must be gently firmed by walking across the plot then raking the surface level. This exercise should be repeated two or three times walking in a different direction each time.

A fine tilth, free from weeds and stones, will eventually develop, ideal for marking out the knot garden pattern.

Nature provides an automatic supply of nutrients to the soil during the 'live, die and decay' process through which all plants progress. A woodland floor is one of the best demonstrations of this cycle as the moist, spongy ground is made up of layers of leaf mould which have decayed over many seasons. As leaves break down they create a natural organic matter, rich in nutrients to feed the soil. In a garden environment this natural process is unavoidably disturbed as maintenance tasks necessitate removal of weeds, leaves and prunings. Pest and diseases often thrive amongst decaying plant material which should generally be cleared from the garden. Additionally, gardeners expect much more from relatively small areas of soil which support large numbers and a wide range of plants. Inevitably nutrient levels reduce and whilst the addition of organic matter each spring contributes in a small way, fertilisers should also be incorporated annually.

Traditionally gardeners would visit plant nurseries to select the stock they wished to buy. This would be reserved for the client then lifted from the ground and despatched through autumn for planting in the dormant season. These days, however, most plants supplied to the public are sold as container grown stock. Well established root balls and a compost rich in nutrients ensures plants are available all year round, in theory extending planting time to twelve months of the year. However it is difficult to improve on the enforced practice of our gardening forebears who carried out major planting work in autumn and winter. At this time the plants are resting and while little top growth develops, roots are able to use available energy to penetrate deep into the soil. If this has been properly prepared, a mass of fine fibrous roots will develop to enable the plant to draw moisture and nutrients from deep in the soil during dry summer months. Strong, anchoring roots will also develop to ensure the plants are physically supported through-

out their life. Planting container grown plants in summer is possible but these often remain shallow rooted, unstable and dependent on false irrigation methods.

If the ideal time for planting is autumn through winter, ground preparation is perfect when carried out in early autumn. At this time of year the soil is still relatively warm, becoming increasingly moist from autumn rain, dew and mist. Once the more severe winter weather develops, heavy soils are almost impossible to cultivate.

**Follow these simple steps to ensure ground is properly prepared for any garden, with particular attention paid to the levelling process for knot gardens.**

*Remove existing plants or turf from the site by digging with a spade or garden fork. On large sites or if serious weed problems prevail, use a chemical herbicide.*

*Rotovate or double dig the whole area to relieve compaction and unearth large stones and roots of perennial weeds, all of which must be removed from site.*

*Incorporate large amounts of organic matter into the soil at this stage, taking care to add it into both subsoil and topsoil. A phosphate rich fertiliser can also be added to the subsoil.*

*Level the ground. Use a landscape rake then walk over the area with small steps.*

*Fork in a fertiliser – a high phosphate feed in autumn and a balanced fertiliser in spring. Always wear gloves.*

*Repeat the levelling and walking process – by this stage the ground will be firm, level and free of unwanted plants and stones.*

# FROM PAGE TO GROUND

The site has now been prepared and it is time to begin transferring the design from paper to ground. This can be a time consuming operation but with patience and perseverance you can accurately copy the design into the garden, in preparation for the long awaited planting work. I find this one of the most exciting stages; seeing the finely raked soil set out with string lines and then watching the design gradually develop. Try and photograph this and each following stage of work as in two or three years time you will find it difficult to remember these early days. You will be like a proud parent looking back through family photographs.

There are two stages to transposing the design from paper to ground; positioning the knot within the garden landscape, then creating your patterns inside the outline shape. Whether or not you have previous experience, the following steps should enable you to carry out both stages with accuracy. If you are working on a very large site or feel unable to tackle the work yourself, you can call in professionals to help. A good firm of landscape contractors should be able to do the work for you, or, in a very large garden, you may need to employ a chartered surveyor to mark out the garden and its internal patterns. Addresses of the professional bodies for landscape contractors and chartered surveyors are listed on page 154.

Lines drawn on paper are transposed into the garden by substituting tape measures for rulers and compasses. Thirty or fifty metre landscape tapes are needed and these are often supplied by hire shops or sold by builders merchants. You will also need an enormous ball or two of twine, wooden pegs and spray paint or sand in a bottle.

A knot garden is often seen from the house and would generally be positioned square to the building. In any surveying practice a permanent feature must be identified, most usually the house in a garden situation. In the larger landscape you might use a tree, fence or telegraph pole. These permanent features are important to ensure you can always return to the site and achieve identical measurements by working from the same fixed point.

Pythagoras's theorem is used to create right-angled triangles and is crucial in setting out any new garden. It is important never to assume a right angle as the eye can deceive, especially outdoors. A right-angled triangle has sides in proportions of 3 : 4 : 5; i.e., a 3 metre long side, a 4 metre long side and a 5 metre long side, or any multiples of 3 : 4 : 5 e.g., 9 : 12 : 15. This exercise should help you to understand the practice as well as the theory.

## A right-angled triangle

*At scale 1:50, draw the horizontal line **ab**, 3 metres long.*
*Set your compass to 4 metres using the same scale and position the point at **a**. Draw arc **ac**.*
*Set your compass to 5 metres using the same scale and position the point at **b**. Draw arc **bc**.*
*Join lines **ac** and **bc** where the arcs cross.*

You have constructed an accurate right-angled triangle.

The same triangle can be created in the garden using landscape tapes as follows.

## A right-angled triangle in the garden

*Set out a line **ab** measuring 3 metres long.*
*Hook the metal ring of the landscape tape to a garden cane then push the cane into the ground at **a**.*

**A right-angled triangle**

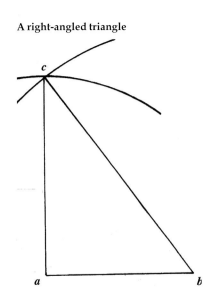

*Run the tape out to 4 metres long and, using sand as a marker, create an arc at point **c**.*

*Hook the metal ring of the landscape tape to a garden cane and push into the ground at point **b**.*

*Run the tape out to 5 metres long and, using sand as a marker, create an arc at point **c**.*

*Using sand, a can of spray paint or string lines attached to canes, create the lines **ac** and **ab** and you have an accurate right-angled triangle on the ground.*

Using this method the following exercise demonstrates how to create a knot garden parallel to a house. We will use scale 1:100 and draw a knot garden which measures 10 metres square, as in previous exercises. The centre of the knot will be directly opposite the front door and the building wall runs from point **x** to **y**. The front door is positioned at **a**.

### Siting the garden in relation to the house

*Measure 3 metres from the front door in both directions along the building wall, marking points **b** and **c**.*

*Set your compass to 5 metres, place the point at **a** and draw a continuous arc, labelled **de**.*

*Set your compass to 4 metres, place the point at **b** and draw an arc to intersect at **d**.*

*Retaining the same compass setting, place the point at **c** and draw an arc to intersect at **e**.*

*Draw line **fg** which runs through points **d** and **e**. This should be 10 metres long to form the base line of your knot garden. Make sure the 5 metre point is directly opposite the front door.*

*To construct the sides of the garden, we will use larger triangles with sides 6, 8 and 10 metres long.*

*Measure 6 metres from point **f** along line **fg**, labelled **h**.*

*Measure 6 metres from point **g** along line **fg**, labelled **i**.*

*Set compass to 10 metres, place point at **h** and draw an arc. Repeat with compass point at **i**.*

*Set compass to 8 metres, place point at **f** and draw an arc. Repeat with compass point at **g**.*

*Draw lines **fj** and **gk**, 10 metres long and running through the crossing arcs as before.*

*Finally draw line **jk** which will also measure 10 metres long.*

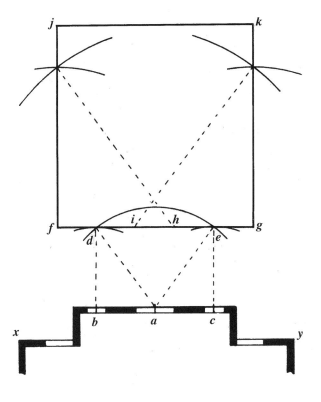

Siting the garden in relation to the house

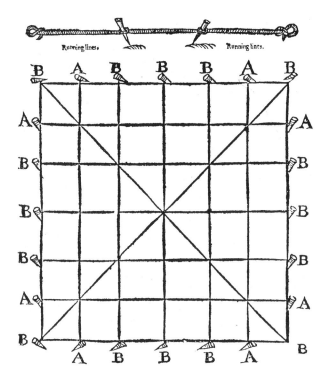

164. A woodcut from the *Maison Rustique* showing the setting out of the ground using pegs and cord lines.

**165. Laying out the knot garden at Morville Dower House. Katherine Swift transfers the pattern from paper to ground using different coloured sands for the various hedges.**

**166. The pattern complete and ready for planting. The planted knot can be seen on pages 54 and 55.**

The same procedure would be followed using landscape tapes to set out the design on the ground.

Once the outline of a design is positioned in the garden, internal lines and patterns must be accurately transposed from the drawing to the ground. Take your mind back to when you were drawing your pattern and develop the design in the same way, using spray paint or sand dribbled from a bottle instead of a pencil.

### Transposing the design

*Insert wooden pegs around the outline shape at 50 cm intervals to correspond to the graph paper grid.*

*Attach string to each peg, running it across to the peg directly opposite to create a string grid of squares, as shown in the woodcut, below left.*

*If you have used circles within the pattern, set another wooden peg at the centre point and use a piece of twine the length of the radius to guide a line of sand.*

*Transpose the design working from a square on the graph paper, accurately copying the pattern to the ground using sand or spray paint.*

Even complicated, freehand patterns can be set out in this way. You may find you need a smaller grid to copy a freehand pattern, perhaps marked out at 25 cm intervals. The weaving threads of the Lovers Knot will fit into a grid but would probably need adjusting by eye. Keep standing back from your work to check the design is developing satisfactorily.

Once the lines have all been drawn, the hedge can be planted. Carefully remove the pegs and lines and begin planting by following the same process as when you were drawing. Plant the outline shape first, spacing the plants between 15 and 20 cm apart, depending on species. If you have an important central plant such as the holly spiral, plant this now, then continue with the next shape you drew taking care that other lines are not disrupted in the process. Build up the pattern in this way until the whole garden is complete.

# FUTURE CARE
# AND MAINTENANCE

Once a knot garden has been planted the first two seasons' care are crucial to ensure strong, healthy plants develop for the future. The worst enemy of any new planting is summer drought and it may be necessary to irrigate the garden throughout the first summer if the weather is hot and dry. It is better to water for a long time once or twice a week than to irrigate for a short time each day. The latter only moistens the upper layers of soil, encouraging surface rooting which risks the roots being burnt during hot spells. The plants are likely to die if this happens. Surface water also evaporates quickly in the sun, wasting much of the water, so irrigate during the evening or through the night on a timed system for a couple of hours. It is important to use an effective system to avoid undue water wastage. Powerful sprinklers on raised tripods are the most wasteful of all so consider some of the seep hose or fine nozzle sprinklers available. Irrigation systems can be installed simply and effectively during the preparation of a garden so decide early on if you wish to invest in such a scheme.

Once the garden has become established, the need to irrigate will be less crucial in terms of plant survival. Good soil preparation ensures hedge roots penetrate deep into the soil, helping the plants survive periods of drought. In particularly hot summers, herbaceous plants may become stressed and possibly susceptible to pest and disease if they are not watered. Usually they recover and the following season show few ill effects, but occasionally the conditions may be so severe that the plants die. In the long term therefore it is important to strike a balance between extravagant water usage and effective irrigation which will ensure the garden looks its best for the longest period possible. Irrigation also means some

herbaceous plants like hardy geraniums and *Astrantia major* can be cut back after flowering and may repeat flower later in summer, but other specimens, for example some bulbs, can deteriorate if a garden is irrigated. In their natural habitat some bulbs are baked dry through the dormant summer season; without this pattern being mimicked, flowering shoots may not develop.

Contrary to appearances, the fully planted knot has relatively low maintenance demands if the ground has been thoroughly prepared and a well planned planting scheme developed. Full planting creates little opportunity for weeds to encroach and ornamental plants generally support one another, avoiding the need for artificial plant supports. Should some plants become damaged by wind or rain or prove softer in their growth than expected, hazel twigs are effective plant supports and less aesthetically offensive than plastic equivalents. Try to leave an unplanted strip as wide as your foot around the hedge to allow access when required. This will enable you to dead head and cut back plants without causing too much damage to other material.

Depending on the size of plants a young box hedge will take a few years to reach its final height and width. During the first two or three years, vertical shoots should be pinched back in early summer to encourage blanched growth from the base. From then on shoots can be allowed to grow longer, but all new growth should be cut back by about a third around mid May. Hedges planted with woody herbs like cotton lavender should be cut back hard in late spring. While this looks brutal, the plants grow quickly and should regain their original height within about six weeks. From then on, clip the hedge lightly through

## CONTACTS

**British Association of Landscape Industries** (BALI)
9 Henry Street, Keighley, West Yorkshire
BD21 3DR. Tel. 01535 606139

**Royal Institution of Chartered Surveyors**
Surveyor Court, West Wood Way,
Coventry CV4 8JE Tel. 01203 694757

**The Building Centre**
26 Store Street, London WC1E 7BT
Tel:0171 637 1022

**Garden History Society**
77 Cowcross Street, London EC1M 6BP
Tel. 0171 608 2409

**Museum of Garden History**
Lambeth Palace Road, London SE1 7LB
Tel. 0171 401 8865

**167. A gardener at Ham House using a conical frame to trim the cones. Sacking on the gravel catches the trimmings.**

of nutrient supply in the garden but more importantly is used for soil improvement, weed suppression and water retention. Many materials can be used as mulch for example:

*Spent mushroom compost*
*Well rotted farmyard manure*
*Well rotted garden compost*
*Spent hops*
*Rotted seaweed*
*Proprietary brands*

As already mentioned, it is important to use large amounts of organic matter during ground preparation, but then continue to apply the same material as an annual mulch. The best time to apply a mulch is early spring, after the winter rains and snow but before growth begins. A 12 cm layer is most effective, acting as a weed suppressant and creating a moisture retentive layer. Worms and soil bacteria will assist in incorporating the material into the soil during the year, thus increasing its bulk and water holding capacity. The process should be repeated each spring.

Different maintenance demands can be expected of the simple knot garden which uses only hedge plants for effect. The soil within compartments may be covered with a layer of ornamental gravel or stone chippings. Lay these over landscape fabric or woven plastic, pegged down with wire to ensure weeds are kept to a minimum but also allowing rainwater to percolate through to the soil. Laying sheets prior to hedge trimming reduces time spent on collecting clippings which look untidy if left on the decorative surface.

If the compartments are to be planted for seasonal interest using bulbs and bedding plants, there will be short bursts of high maintenance work as each season changes. Winter flowering pansies and spring flowering tulips can be removed in late April or early May and, after the last frost, summer bedding can be planted. This should be removed and replaced again with pansies and bulbs in October or November. Regular weeding, feeding and irrigation is required for seasonal bedding displays.

summer whenever it begins to look untidy. Do not cut at all after the end of August as early frost could damage the plants. Other woody herbs like lavender and rosemary are generally more reluctant to grow new shoots from old wood. Give a shaping cut in late spring, removing untidy wood from the previous year, but do not cut into older shoots. Rosemary can be lightly trimmed whenever it begins to look untidy but lavender only needs faded flower stems removed in late summer.

The fully planted knot garden demands much from the soil in terms of nutrients so it is important to replenish the natural resources regularly. Pelleted chicken manure is effective and quite cheap. If the garden looks weary during summer, a quick release fertiliser can be given in liquid form, either watered into damp soil or sprayed on to foliage in the evening. Organic seaweed feed is useful. There are also many specialist, proprietary brands of in-organic fertilisers on the market and slow release pellets which feed the garden throughout a whole season are useful, although expensive. Mulching can be a form

# GARDENS TO VISIT

Although not exhaustive the following list includes gardens with knots, parterres and other features that are of particular relevance to readers of this book. They are generally open to the public but some only infrequently, for example with the National Gardens Scheme (NGS).

**Antony**, Torpoint, Cornwall (National Trust). Recent knot of box and germander. Tel. 01752 812191.

**Ashdown House**, nr Lambourn, Oxfordshire (National Trust). A fine 17th-century-style box parterre. Tel. 01488 72584.

**Barnsley House**, nr Cirencester, Gloucestershire (Mr Charles Verey). Knot garden and potager created by Rosemary Verey. Tel. 01285 740281.

**Basing House**, Basingstoke, Hampshire (Hampshire County Council). Recreated 16th-17th-century formal gardens. Tel. 01256 467294.

**31 Bassett Crescent West**, Southampton, Hampshire (Bryan and Angela Hunt). Sculpture knot garden designed by Johnny Woodford. Tel. 01703 790628

**Blenheim Palace**, Oxfordshire (His Grace the Duke of Marlborough). Exotic water parterre of the early 20th century. Tel. 01993 811325.

**Bodrhyddan**, Rhuddan, Denbighshire (Lord Langford). Formal garden and Nesfield parterre. Tel. 01745 590414.

**Bodysgallen Hall**, Llandudno, North Wales (Historic House Hotels). Late 19th-century walled parterre planted with herbs. Tel. 01492 584466.

**Boscobel House**, Shropshire (English Heritage). Historic 17th-century box garden and mount. Tel. 01902 850244.

**1 Brook Cottages**, East Meon, Hampshire (Mr and Mrs D.Stapley). Knot of culinary and physic herbs. Tel. 01730 823376 (NGS and by appointment).

**Broughton Castle**, nr Banbury, Oxfordshire (Lord Saye and Sele). Fleur-de-lis knot in the Ladies' Garden. Tel. 01295 262624.

**Broughton Hall**, nr Skipton, Yorkshire (Mr H.R.Tempest). Nesfield parterre. Tel. 01756 792267.

**Castle Ashby**, Northamptonshire (Marquess of Northampton). Victorian terraced garden. Tel. 01604 696696.

**Chenies Manor House**, Buckinghamshire (Lt Col. and Mrs Macleod Matthews). Formal sunken garden and mazes. Tel. 01494 762888.

**Chevening**, nr Sevenoaks, Kent (By permission of the Board of Trustees of Chevening Estate and The Secretary of State for Foreign and Commonwealth Affairs). Maze and parterre. (NGS).

**Claverton Manor**, nr Bath, Somerset (The American Museum in Britain). Replica of George Washington's box garden at Mount Vernon. Tel. 01225 460503.

**Cressing Temple**, nr Braintree, Essex. Modern garden based on late 15th and early 16th-century gardens, including knots and medieval features. Tel. 01376 584903.

**Ditchley Park**, Enstone, Oxfordshire (Ditchley Foundation). Parterres in formal design by Geoffrey Jellicoe. Tel. 01608 677346.

**Drummond Castle Gardens**, Perthsire, Scotland (Grimsthorpe and Drummond Castle Trust). Magnificent 19th-century parterres. Tel. 01764 681257.

**Dunrobin Castle**, Sutherland, Scotland (The Countess of Sutherland). Charles Barry parterres. Tel. 01408 633177.

**Edzell Castle**, Tayside, Scotland (Historic Scotland). Outstanding recreation of a Renaissance garden. Tel. 01356 648631.

**Ham House**, Richmond, London (National Trust). 17th-century style garden. Tel. 0181 940 1950.

**Hampton Court Palace**, London (Historic Royal Palaces). Restored Privy Garden. Tudor knot garden recreated by Ernest Law early in 20th century. Tel. 0181 781 9500.

**Hanbury Hall**, Worcestershire (National Trust). Recreation of London and Wise formal garden with sunken parterre. Tel. 01527 821214.

**Harewood House**, nr Leeds, Yorkshire (Harewood House Trust). Victorian terrace with parterres. Tel. 0113 2886331.

**Hatfield House**, Hertfordshire (The Marquess of Salisbury). Knot garden and parterres designed by Lady Salisbury. Tel. 01707 262823.

**Helmingham Hall Gardens**, Stowmarket, Suffolk (Lord and Lady Tollemache). Moated garden with knot containing plants grown in England before 1750. Tel. 01473 890363.

**Hestercombe Gardens**, nr Taunton, Somerset (Somerset County Council and the Hestercombe Gardens Project Ltd). Lutyens/Jekyll 'Great Plat'. Tel. 01823 413923.

**Hexham Herbs**, nr Hexham, Northumberland (Mr and Mrs K.White). National thyme collection and knot garden. Tel. 01434 681483.

**Holkham Hall**, Wells, Norfolk (The Earl of Leicester). Extensive parterres laid out by William Nesfield. Tel. 01328 710277.

**Hollington Herbs**, nr Newbury, Berkshire (Mr and Mrs S.G.Hopkinson). Herb nursery with ornamental garden including recent knots. Tel. 01635 253908.

**Holme Pierrepont Hall**, nr Nottingham, Nottinghamshire (Mr and Mrs Robin Brackenbury). Courtyard garden with box parterre. Tel. 0115 9332371.

**Ickworth**, nr Bury St Edmunds, Suffolk (National Trust). Formal gardens and collection of *Buxus*. Tel. 01284 735270.

**Langley Boxwood Nursery**, nr Liss, Hampshire ((Mrs Elizabeth Brainbridge). Specialist box suppliers with national collection of *Buxus*. Tel. 01730 894467.

**Little Moreton Hall**, Congleton, Cheshire (National Trust). Recreated knot garden based on a 17th-century design. Tel. 01260 272018.

**Mellerstain**, Gordon, Borders Region, Scotland (The Mellerstain Trust). Fine terrace garden with parterre laid out by Blomfield at beginning of 20th century. Tel. 01573 410225.

**Morville Gardens**, nr Bridgnorth, Shropshire, The Dower House has fine Elizabethan knot garden designed by Dr Katherine Swift. Tel. 01746 714407.

**Moseley Old Hall**, nr Woverhampton, Staffordshire (National Trust). Fine 17th-century knot garden based on the design of the Revd Walter Stonehouse. Tel. 01902 782808.

**Mottisfont Abbey**, nr Romsey, Hampshire (National Trust). Superb rose gardens and knot garden. Tel. 01794 340757.

**Museum of Garden History**, Lambeth, London (The Tradescant Trust). Recreated 17th-century garden with knot design by Lady Salisbury. Tel. 0171 401 8865.

**Museum of Welsh Life**, St Fagan's Castle, Cardiff. Modern knot garden based on 17th-century designs. Tel. 01222 573500.

**New Place**, Stratford-upon-Avon, Warwickshire (Shakespeare Birthplace Trust). Grounds of Shakespeare's last home with a colourful Elizabethan-style garden recreated in the 20th century by Ernest Law. Tel. 01789 414372.

**Oxburgh Hall**, Swaffham, Norfolk (National Trust). A French style parterre laid out in the mid 19th century. Tel. 01366 328258.

**Penrhyn Castle**, Bangor, Gwynedd, Wales (National Trust). Victorian formal garden. Tel. 01248 353084.

**Penshurst Place**, nr Tunbridge Wells, Kent (Viscount De L'Isle). Large formal gardens with colourful parterres. Tel. 01892 870307.

**Pitmedden Garden**, Grampian Region, Scotland (National Trust for Scotland). Reconstructed 17th-century garden with elaborate parterres. Tel. 01651 842352.

**Red Lodge**, Bristol (Bristol City Council). Recreated early 17th-century town garden. Tel. 0117 9211360.

**Regent's Park**, London (Royal Parks Agency). Part of Nesfield's designs have recently been restored.

**Rousham House**, Oxfordshire (Mr C. Cottrell-Dormer). Small parterre by pigeon house. Tel. 01869 347110.

**Somerleyton Hall**, nr Lowestoft, Suffolk (The Lord and Lady Somerleyton). Now only the site of a Nesfield parterre but the magnificent maze survives. Tel. 01502 732950.

**Sudeley Castle**, Winchcombe, Gloucestershire (Lord and Lady Ashcombe). Recreated knot garden with water features. Tel. 01242 602308.

**Tollemache Hall**, Offton, Suffolk (Mr and Mrs M.Tollemache). Knot garden (NGS).

**Tredegar House**, Newport, Wales (Newport County Borough Council). Recently restored early 18th-century parterres. Tel. 01633 815880.

**Tudor Garden**, Tudor House Museum, Southampton, Hampshire (Southampton City Council). A new Tudor garden designed and planted by Dr Sylvia Landsberg. Tel. 01703 332513.

**Waterperry Gardens**, nr Wheatley, Oxfordshire (School of Economic Science). Newly designed and planted knot garden. Tel. 01844 339254.

**Yalding Organic Gardens**, Yalding, Kent (HDRA). Woven knot using hyssop. Tel. 01622 814650.

# BIBLIOGRAPHY

## CONTEMPORARY WORKS

**Alberti**, Leon Battista, *De Re Aedificatoria*. Florence,1485 [First English translation *The Ten Books of Architecture*, 1755].

**Anon**, *The Expert Gardener* [bound with *The Country-mans Recreation*]. London, 1640.

**Anon**, *The Orchard and the Garden*. London, 1594.

**Anon**, *A Short Instruction Verie Profitable and Necessarie for All Those that Delight in Gardening*. London, 1591.

**Bacon**, Francis, *Essays* [including *Of Gardens*]. London, 1625.

**Blake**, Stephen, *The Compleat Gardeners Practice*. London, 1664.

**Boyceau de la Barauderie**, Jacques, *Traité du Jardinage*. Paris, 1638.

**Camden**, William, *Britannia*, 1586.

**Caus**, Isaac de, *Le Jardin de Wilton*. c.1645.

**Colonna**, Francesco, *Hypnerotomachia Poliphili*. Venice, 1499 [French edition, 1546].

**De Vries**, Hans Vredeman, *Hortorum Viridariorumque Elegantes….*Antwerp, 1583.

**Du Cerceau**, Jacques Androuet, *Les Plus Excellents Bastiments de France*. 1576.

**Estienne**, Charles [and] **Liébault**, J., *L'Agriculture et Maison Rustique*. Paris, 1570 [enlarged edition with knot designs, 1586].

**Estienne**, Charles [and] **Liébault**, J., *Maison Rustique, or The Countrie Farme*, trans. Richard **Surflet**. London, 1600.

**Estienne**, Charles [and] **Liébault**, J., *Maison Rustique or The Countrey Farme*, enlarged by Gervase **Markham**. London, 1616.

**Ferris**, C. F., *The Parterre*. 1837.

**Gedde** [or **Gidde**], Walter, *Booke of Sundry Draughtes, Principally Serving for Glaziers: and not Impertinent for Plasterers and Gardiners besides Sundry Other Professions*. London, 1615.

**Hanmer**, Thomas, *The Garden Book of Sir Thomas Hanmer*; with an introduction by Eleanour Sinclair Rohde. London, 1933.

**Hawes**, Stephen, *The Passetime of Pleasure*. London, 1509.

**Hentzner**, Paul, *A Journey into England…in the year MDXCVIII*. Strawberry Hill, 1757.

**Hill** [or **Hyll**], Thomas, *A Most Briefe and Pleasaunte Treatyse….*London, [1558?].

**Hill**, Thomas, *The Proffitable Arte of Gardening….* London, 1568.

**Hill**, Thomas, *The Gardeners Labyrinth*. London, 1577. [Published under the pseudonym Didymus Mountain].

**James**, John, *The Theory and Practice of Gardening*. London, 1712. [Translation of **Dezallier d'Argenville**, *La Théorie et la Pratique du Jardinage*. Paris, 1709].

**Jonson**, Ben, *Pleasure Reconciled to Virtue* (1618) in *The Works of Ben Jonson*, Volume 5. London, 1716.

**Knyff**, Leonard [and] **Kip**, Johannes, *Brittania Illustrata*. London, 1720.

**Langley**, Batty, *New Principles of Gardening, or the Laying out and Planting of Parterres*. London, 1728.

**Lawson**, William, *A New Orchard and Garden*. London, 1618. [Including *The Countrie Housewifes Garden*, 1617].

**Loggan**, David, *Oxonia Illustrata*. Oxford, 1675.

**London**, George [and] **Wise**, Henry, *The Retir'd Gard'ner*. London, 1706. [Translation of **Gentil**, F., *Le Jardinier Solitaire*, 1704, and **Liger**, L., *Le Jardinier Fleuriste*, 1706].

**Loris**, Daniel, *Le Thrésor des Parterres de l'Univers*. Geneva, 1629.

**Loudon**, John Claudius, *The Suburban Gardener*. London, 1838.

**Markham**, Gervase, *The English Husbandman*. London, 1613-15.

**Meager**, Leonard, *The English Gardener*. London, 1670.

**M'Intosh**, *The Flower Garden*. New edition, London 1839.

**Mollet**, André, *Le Jardin de Plaisir*. Stockholm, 1651.

**Mollet**, Claude, *Théâtre des Plans et Jardinages*. 1652.

**Parkinson**, John, *Paradisi in Sole Paradisus Terrestris*. London, 1629.

**Platter**, Thomas, *Travels in England, 1599*, translated by Clare Williams. London, 1937.

**Rye**, William B., *England as Seen by Foreigners*. London, 1865

**Serlio**, Sebastiano, *The Five Books of Architecture*. English edition, London, 1611.

**Serres**, Olivier de, *Le Théâtre d'Agriculture et Mesnage des Champs*. Paris, 1600.

**Switzer**, Stephen, *Ichnographia Rustica*. London, 1718.

**Van der Groen**, *Le Jardinier de Pays-Bas*. Brussels, 1681.

**Whitney**, G., *A choice of Emblems and other Devises*. Leyden, 1586.

**Wilkinson**, Gardner, *On Colour and on the necessity for a general diffusion of taste among all classes*. London, 1858.

## MODERN SOURCES

**Allen**, J. Romilly, *Celtic Art, in Pagan and Christian Times*. Methuen, 1904.

**Amherst**, Alicia, *A History of Gardening in England*. Quaritch, 1895.

**Anthony**, John, *Discovering Period Gardens*. Shire, 1972.

**Bain**, Iain, *Celtic knotwork*. Constable, 1986.

**Beck**, Thomasina, *Gardening with Silk and Gold: A history of gardens in embroidery*. David & Charles, 1997.

**Binney**, Marcus and **Hills**, Anne, *Elysian Gardens*. Save Britain's Heritage, 1979.

**Blomfield**, Reginald, *The Formal Garden in England*. London, 1892.

**Boyle**, E.V., *Days and Hours in a Garden*. Second edition, 1884.

**Cirlot**, J. E., *A Dictionary of Symbols*. Routledge & Kegan Paul, 1962.

**Clifford**, Derek, *A History of Garden Design*. Faber, 1962.

**Cole**, Nathen, *The Royal Parks and Gardens of London*. London, 1877.

**Crisp**, Frank, *Mediaeval Gardens*. 1924.

**Dent**, John, *The Quest for Nonsuch*. Rev. ed.. Hutchinson, 1970.

**Ellacombe**, Henry N., *The Plant-Lore and Garden-Craft of Shakespeare*. 1878.

**Elliott**, Brent, *Victorian Gardens*. Batsford, 1986.

**Freeman**, Rosemary, *English Emblem Books*. Chatto & Windus, 1948.

**Griswold**, Mac and **Weller**, Eleanor, *The Golden Age of American Gardens*. N.Y.: Abrams, 1991.

**Gunther**, R.T., 'The gardens of the Rev. Walter Stonehouse at Darfield Rectory in Yorkshire, 1640'. *Gardeners Chronicle*, 1920, i, pp.240-41,256,268,296.

**Harvey**, John, *Early Nurserymen, with reprints of documents and lists*. Phillimore, 1974.

**Harvey**, John, *Mediaeval Gardens*. Batsford, 1981.

**Henrey**, Blanche, *British Botanical and Horticultural Literature before 1800*. O.U.P., 1975. 3v.

**Hobhouse, Penelope,** *Plants in Garden History*. Pavilion, 1992.

**Hunt**, John Dixon and **Willis**, Peter, *The Genius of the Place: The English landscape garden 1620-1820*. Elek, 1975.

**Institute of Advanced Architectural Studies, The University of York**, *William Andrew Nesfield: Victorian Landscape Architect*: Papers from the Bicentenary Conference, The King's Manor, York, 1994; edited by Christopher Ridgway. 1996.

**Johnson**, Francis R., 'Thomas Hill: an Elizabethan Huxley'. *Huntington Library Quarterly*, 4 (August 1944)

**Johnson**, George W., *A History of English Gardening*. London, 1829.

**Kerr**, Robert, *The Gentleman's House*. London, 1864.

**Kipling**, Gordon, *The Triumph of Honour*. Leiden U.P., 1977.

**Landsberg**, Sylvia, *The Medieval Garden*. British Museum Press, 1995.

**Law**, Ernest, *Hampton Court Gardens: Old and New*. London, 1926.

**Lazzaro**, Claudia, *The Italian Renaissance Garden*. Yale U.P., 1990.

**Lethaby**, W. R., *Mediaeval Art*. Revised edition, Duckworth, 1912.

**Matthews**, W. H., *Mazes and Labyrinths*. Longmans, 1922.

**Robinson**, William, *The Wild Garden*. London, 1870.

**Rohde**, Eleanor Sinclair, *The Old English Gardening Books*. Hopkinson, 1924.

**Rykwert**, Joseph, *The First Moderns*. MIT Press, 1980.

**Sedding**, John D., *Garden-Craft Old and New*. London, 1891.

**Singer**, S.W., *The Life of Cardinal Wolsey*. Chiswick, 1825.

**Strong**, Roy, *The Renaissance Garden in England*. Thames & Hudson, 1979.

**Sturdy**, David, 'The Tradescants at Lambeth', *Journal of Garden History*, 2, 1982, the garden at Darfield, pp.5-9.

**Thacker**, Christopher, *The Genius of Gardening*. Weidenfeld & Nicolson, 1994.

**Thurley**, Simon, *The Royal Palaces of Tudor England*. Yale U.P., 1993.

**Triggs**, H. Inigo, *Formal Gardens in England and Scotland*. Batsford, 1902.

**Verey**, Rosemary, 'Knots and Parterres: a bibliography'. *Garden History*, Vol.2, no.2 (1974).

**Walters**, Michael, *The Garden in Victorian Literature*. Scolar, 1988.

**Wind**, Edgar, *Pagan Mysteries in the Renaissance*. Rev. ed., Faber, 1968.

**Woodbridge**, Kenneth, *Princely Gardens*. Thames & Hudson, 1986.

agapanthus 100, **157**
Ahenny 21
Alberti, Leon Battista 27, 33, 38, 44, 140, **23**
Alexander the Great 15
All Souls College 48, 49, **53**
Allen, Romilly 20
alleys 31, 32, 37, 53, 61, 64, **21**, **32**, **36**
alliums 130, 138
Alnwick 30
alpines 101
Amboise 29, 32, 36
Ambrogiana, The 33, 46, **21**
American Museum in Britain 92
Amherst, Alicia 30, 56
Amport 86
anemones 121
*Anenome blanda* 119
*Anethum graveolens* 139
Anglo-Dutch garden 68
Anne, Queen 70
annuals 78, 111, 123
aquilegia **154**
arbours 27, 32, 37, 46, 49, 61, 65, 101, 106, **21**
Ariadne 15
*Armeria maritima* 117
Arthur, Prince 29
Arts and Crafts Movement 77, 84, 86, 89
Art Workers' Guild 84
Arundel House 59
*Astrantia major* 128, 154
Athelhampton 77, 86
Augustine, Saint 20
azaleas 148
Bacon, Francis 54, 84
Bain, Iain 22
balm, lemon 40, 138
Barnsley House 13, 92, 112, 142, **140**
Barry, Sir Charles 77-79
bay 70, 99
beans 136
Beaton, Donald 81
bedding schemes 78, 92, 104, 155
Benthall Hall 54
*Berberis buxifolia* 'Nana' 117
*Bergenia cordifolia* 103, **135**
Bettisfield 62
biennials 111, 123-24
Binney, Marcus 79
bird's-eye view 44, 45, 59, 74, **91**, **98**
Birr Castle 112
Blake, Stephen 13, 61, 62, 66, 92, 112,

142, 146, **2**, **77**
Blenheim Palace 88, **100**
Blois 29, 36, 46, **30**
Blomfield, Reginald 77, 86, 88
Bodrhyddan 84
Bodysgallen Hall 86, 131, **119**
Boleyn, Anne 32, 33
Book of Kells 20
*Booke of Sundry Draughtes* 53, **18**
Boscobel House 66, **83-85**, **162**
Boston House 61, **75**
Bouts, Dirck 22, 24, **15**
box (*Buxus*) 38, 43, 52, 53, 54, 56, 61, 62, 65, 66, 68, 70, 73, 81, 82, 86, 88, 89, 92, 98, 99, 100, 101, 104, 107, 111-113, 115, 117, 119, 124, 142, **42**, **144**, **145**, **155**
Boyceau, Jacques 62
Boyle, E.V. 84
*British Botanical and Horticultural Literature before 1800* 66
Brompton Park nurseries 70
Broughton Castle 86, **118**, **153**, **159**
Broughton Hall 82, **111-13**, 141
Brown, 'Capability' 7
Bruce, Sir William 68, 73
Buckingham, 3rd Duke of *see* Stafford, Edward
bulbs 100, 104, 111, 119, 130, 154, 155, **146-49**, **157**
Burgundian courts 29
Burrell Collection, 19
*Buxus, see* box 112
Byzantine art 20, 24
caduceus 17
*Calendula officinalis* 124
Camden, William 37
campion 124, 126
candytuft 124
cannas 132
carnations 117, 128
carpet bedding 84, 128
carpet page 19, 10
Cartwright, Joseph 84
*Caryopteris* x *clandonensis* 'Heavenly Blue' 117
Castle Ashby 78, 109
Caus, Isaac de 60, 61, 74
Cavendish, George 32
Cecil, Robert 61
Cecil, Thomas 56
Cecil, William, Lord Burghley 54
cedar 28
ceiling mouldings 43, 45, **75**, **106**

Celtic art 20-22, 49, 93, 140, **11**, **14**
Chambers, Sir William 7
chamomile 28, 52, 53, 117
Charles II 68
Charles VIII 29, 32
Charles, Prince 65, 66
chartered surveyors 151
Chartres Cathedral 15, 47, **8**
Chatelherault 74
Chaucer, Geoffrey 38
Chelsea Flower Show 92
Chenies Manor **147**, **149**
chincherinchee 132
chives 138
Christian art 15, 19, 20
Christmas rose 117
Cirlot, Juan Eduardo 24
Claverton Manor 92
clematis 136-37
*Clematis flammula* 107
Clifford, Derek 50, 68
climbers 111, 136-37
Cole, Nathan 84
Colonna, Francis 28, 29
columbine 128
Columella 43
*compartiment de broderie* 52, 68
*Compleat Gardeners Practice* 13, 61, 62, 66, 92, **2**, **77**
*Contemplation of Mankinde* 43
cornflowers 123
cotoneaster 117
*Cottage Gardener* 81
cotton lavender 44, 101, 114-16, 142, 144
*Countrie Housewifes Garden* 22, 53, **68**, **71**
*Country-mans Recreation* 49
Crete 15
Crewe Hall 81-83, **108**
crocus 65, 121
crown imperial 65, **148**
Cupid 15, 3
curry plant 115, 116
Curtis, William 144
cut-work 48, 66, 70, 72, 73, 92, 144, **96**
cyclamen 121
cypress 29, 56, 64
Daedalus 15
daffodil 119, 120
dahlias 132
Darfield Rectory 62, 79
*De Re Aedificatoria* 27, 28, 140
De Vries, Vredeman 46, **32**
Delos 15
delphinium 124
Delves, Sir George 55
Dent, John 37
design 140-43
Dethicke, Henry 43, 48
Dezallier d'Argenville, A.-J. 72
*Dianthus* 128-29
*Dictamnus albus* 'Purpureus' **151**
digging 148-49
dill 138, 139

*Discovering Period Gardens* 90
Ditchley Park 92, **122**
Dixon Hunt, John 74
Drumlanrig Castle 78
Drummond Castle 78, **101**
Du Cerceau, Androuet 29, 32, 46, 106, **30**, **33**
Duchêne, Achille 76, 88
Dunrobin 78, **103**
Dyrham Park 70, **91**
*Early Nurserymen* 38
Edzell Castle 90, **123**
Egerton, Lady 84
Elizabeth I, Queen 37, 54, **60**
Elizabeth, Princess 45, 46, 108
Ellacombe, Henry 88
Elliott, Brent 83
*Elysian Gardens* 79
emblems 52
embroidery 37, 45, 46, 48, 49, 50, 54, 59, 61, 64, 70., 72, 73, **34**, **39**, **54**
*Encyclopaedia of Gardening* 77
*English Gardener* 66, 68, **86**
*English Husbandman* 52, **62**
*entrelacs* 50
eremurus 132
Este, Ippolito d' 29
Este, Isabella d' 16
Este, Villa d' 29
Estienne, Charles 49
*Eucomis autumnalis* 132
*Euonymus fortunei* 'Emerald Gaiety' 117
euphorbia **148**
Evelyn, John 68
evening primrose 124
Eworth, Hans **33**
*Expert Gardener* 49
*Family of Henry VIII* 33, **35**
fennel 139
Ferrara, Renée Duchess of 29
Ferris, C.F. 77
fertiliser 114, 147, 150, 154
Field of the Cloth of Gold 32
fleur-de-lis 48, 74, 86, **99**, **118**
*Flower Garden* 77, **102**
*Flower Garden Displayed* 144
*Foeniculum vulgare* 'Purpureum' 138-39
Foley, Lady Emily 82, 83
Fontainebleau 29, 36
forget-me-nots 121
*Formal Garden in England* 77, 86
*Formal Gardens* 68
Fortis Green 80
foxglove 124, **151**
foxtail lily 132
Francis I 29, 32, 36
*Frette, The* 53, **71**
fritillary 120, **148**
fuchsia 128, **155**
Gaillon 32
gallery 29, 30, 31, 32, 33, 44, 46, 64, 106, **27**, **32**
Garden at the Ark, The 132, 137

Garden History Society 90, 92, 144
*Garden of Pleasure* 62
*Garden, The* 88
*Garden-Craft Old and New* 86
*Gardener's Magazine* 77, 80
*Gardeners Labyrinth* 7, 17, 43, 45, 46, 47, 48, 52, 53, 54, 64, 65, 84, 142, **56**, **57**, **58**, **80**
*Gardeners' Chronicle* 62, 84, **108**
Gawthorpe Hall 78, **105**, **106**
*gazon coupé* 70, 72, 92
Gedde, Walter 24, 53, **18**, **40**
Gentil, Francois 70
*Gentleman's House* 77
*Geranium macrorrhizum* **152**
*Geranium tuberosum* 121
geranium, hardy 121, 127-28, 154
Gerard, John 38, 59, 144
germander 43, 53, 54, 61, 66, 112, 115, 116, 142
gillyflower 53, 117, 128
gladiolus 131
Glazier Psalter 24
*Golden Age of American Gardens* 92
golden rod 126
Gordium 15
Gothic art 22, 24, 27, 53, **15**, **16**
Gothic Revival 77
gravel 107, 147
Greber, Jacques 92
Greek art 15, 17
Griswold, Mac 92
ground preparation 147-50
Guernsey lily 132
guilloche 15, 81, 84, **13**
Haddon Hall **37**
Ham House 68, 138, **title-page**, **144**, **167**
Hamilton, Geoff 113
Hampton Court 29, 32, 33, 36, 44, 59, 68, 70, 74, 88, 89, **36**, **72**, **98**, **99**, **134**, **150**
*Hampton Court Gardens* 89
Hanmer, Thomas 62
Harbour Hill 92
hard landscaping 106, **136**
Hardwick Hall 38, 84
Harvey, John 29, 38
Hatfield House 7-9, 61, 92, 97, 101, 129, 144, *figure i*, **1**, **59**, **127**, **128**, **136**, **138**, **145**, **148**, **154**
Hatton, Sir Christopher 90
Hawes, Stephen 30
*Hedera helix* 'Ivalace' 117
hedges 111-17, 141, 144, 153, 154, **140-44**
*Helichrysum angustifolium* 115, 116
hellebores 117, 126, **145**, **148**
Helmingham plan 68
Henrey, Blanche 66
Henry Doubleday Organic Gardens 114
Henry IV 62
Henry VII 29
Henry VIII 29-33, 36, 45, **34**

Hentzner, Paul 37, 56
hepaticas 65
heraldic beasts 37, **36**
heraldry 32, 52
herbaceous plants 97, 114, 154
*Herball, The* 38, 144, **42**
herbs 37, 54, 64, 92, 101, 104, 111, 115, 116, 138-39
Hermes 17
*Hesperis matronalis* 124
Hestercombe 'Great Plat' 103, **135**
Het Loo 68
Hill, Thomas 7, 17, 34, 37, 40, 43-49, 52-54, 57, 77, 83, 84, 86, 89, 97, 101, 142, **48**
*History of English Gardening* 77
*History of Garden Design* 50, 68
*History of Gardening in England* 56
Holbein, Hans 34
Holkham Hall 83
Hollar, Wenceslaus 65, **83**
holly 70, 103, 117, 120
Holmes, Caroline 114
Holyroodhouse, Palace of 72, 73, **94**
honesty 124
honeysuckle 50
hornbeam 106
*Hortorum Viridariumque Elegantes* **32**
Hovenden map 48, 49, **53**
Huntercombe Manor 84
Hunterston brooch 21, **11**
*Huntington Library Quarterly* 43
*Hypnerotomachia Poliphili* 24, 28, 38, 40, 48, **22, 24-26**
hyssop 28, 40, 43, 44, 45, 47, 52, 53, 61, 66, 114
*Iberis umbellata* 124
*Ichnographia Rustica* 92
illuminated manuscripts 19, 20, 24, 27, 48, **10, 16**
*Impatiens* 122
*In a Gloucestershire Garden* 88
iris 131-32, **156**
Iron Age decoration 20
irrigation 154
Italian Renaissance garden 29, **21**
*Italian Renaissance Garden* 38
Italo-Byzantine art 20, 21, 24, **12**
*Itinerary* 31, 33, 36
ivy 88
James II 68
James, John 71, 72, 82, **93, 95, 96**
*Jardin de Plaisir* 64, **82**
*Jardin de Wilton* 61, 66
Jellicoe, Geoffrey 92
Johnson, George 77
Jones, Inigo 44, 59, 61
Jonson, Ben 15
Jourdain, Margaret 40
*Journal of Horticulture and Cottage Gardener* 84
*Justice of the Emperor Otto* **15**
Katherine of Aragon 29
Kennedy, Lewis and George 78
Kent, William 7

Kerr, Robert 77
Kew Gardens 81, 90
Kip, Johannes 59, **91, 98**
Kipling, Gordon 29
Kirby Hall 90
Knole 48, **45**
Knyff, Leonard 59, 74
*L'Agriculture et Maison Rustique, see Maison Rustique*
labyrinth 15, 17, 37, 47, 64, 65, **5, 20**
Lambeth 61
*Lamium maculatum* 'White Nancy' 132
Landsberg, Sylvia 90, 101
landscape contractors 151
landscape fabric 107, 154
landscape garden, English 68, 73, 74
landscape tapes 151
Lapworth Missal 24, **16**
larkspur 124
laurel 28, 70
lavender 28, 40, 44, 53, 54, 89, 102, 106, 114, 116, 138, **137, 144, 152, 162**
Law, Ernest 88, 89
Lawson, William 22, 52, 53, 57, 86, **68, 71**
Lazzarro, Claudia 38
Le Nôtre, André 68, 73
*Le Thrésor des Parterres de l'Univers* 59
Leland, John 31, 33, 36
Lenten rose 117
Leonardo da Vinci 25, 29
*Les Plus Excellents Bastiments de France* 29, 46
lettuce 138, **161, 163**
levelling 148-49
Liébault, Jean 49
Liger, Louis 70
lilies 100, 132
lily beetle 132
lily-of-the-valley 28
Lindisfarne Gospels 19, 20, **10**
Lindsay, Sir David 90
Little Moreton Hall 29, 68, 90, **41, 43, 87, 88, 142**
lobelia 123
*Lobelia cardinalis* 65
Loggan, David 52, 64, 65, **81**
London, George 70, **90**
Longford Castle 78
*Lonicera nitida* 117
Loris, D. 59
Loudon, John Claudius 77, 80
Louis XII 29, 32
Louis XIV 68, 76
Louvre 62
*Love's Labour's Lost* 54
love-in-a-mist 124
*Lozenges* 53, **71**
Ludstone Hall 84, **117**
Lumley, Lord 36, 37
*Lunaria biennis* 124
Luttrell carpet 19, **9**
Lutyens/Jekyll 103, **135**

lychnis 65
Lyte, Henry 38
M'Intosh, Charles 77, **102**
*Maison Rustique* 48-49, 50, 52-54, 57, 59, 66, 77, 78, 83, **63, 164**
Maltese Cross 127 manure 149
marigolds 28, 123, 124
marjoram 28, 40, 44, 52, 61, 117
Markham, Gervase 52, 53, 66, 86, 92
martagon lilies 65
Marvel of Peru 132
Mary Queen of Scots 38
Mary, Queen 68, 74
masterwort 128
maze 15, 17, 44, 45, 46, 47, 53, 54, 83, **49**
Meager, Leonard 66, 68, **86**
medieval architecture 27
medieval garden 24, 27, 106, **19**
Mellerstain 86, **120**
Mercigliano, Pacello de 29
Middle Ages 27, 28
Miles, Paul 101, **129, 130, 152**
*Mina lobata* 136
Minos, King 15
Minotaur 15
*Mirabilis jalapa* 132
Miramar 92
Modena, Nicholas 36
Mollet, André 52, 62, 71
Mollet, Claude 49, 52, 61, 62, 64, **82**
monogram 17, 32, 83, **38**
morning glory 136
Morville Dower House 54, 57, **65, 67, 161, 163, 165, 166**
mosaic 107, 108, **139**
mosaic, Roman 15, 20, 81, **13**
Moseley Old Hall 62, 64, **78, 137**
*Most Briefe and Pleasaunt Treatyse* 43, 44, **47**
Mottisfont Abbey 126
mount 64, 65, **81, 83, 85**
Mountain, Didymus 47
mulch 114, 154
mullein 124
Museum of Garden History 9, 13, 61, 97, 101, 103, 111, 114, 120, 126, 132, 134, 136, 144, 145, 147, **125, 126, 146, 151, 158**
myrtle 40
*Names of Herbes*, 38
Naples 29
narcissus 65, 119, 120
nasturtiums 65, 139
National Trust 73, 90, 136
*Nectaroscordum siculum* 131
*Nerine bowdenii* 132
Nesfield, Markham 84
Nesfield, W.E. 84
Nesfield, William 80-84, **115**
New College, Oxford 52, 64, 65, **81**
*New Orchard and Garden* 53, **70**
New Place, Stratford 88, **121**
*Nigella damascena* 124
Nonsuch 33, 36, 37, 44, **37**

Northampton, 4th Marquess of 81
nutrients 150, 154
*Oenothera biennis* 124
*Of Gardens* 54
*Old English Gardening Books* 46
*On Colour and on the necessity…* 79, **107**
*Onopordum acanthium* 101
*Orchard and the Garden* 49, 61
organic matter 147, 149, 154
*Ornithagalum* 132
pansies 28, 121, 155
*Paradisi in Sole Paradisus Terrestris* 59, **73**
Parkinson, John 9, 59, 60, 61, 62, 93
Parr, Katherine 45, 46
*parterre de broderie* 60, 61, 64, 68, 74, 88, 92, **74, 76, 82**
parterre definition 50
*Parterre, The* 77
*Passetime of Pleasure* 30
paths 101, 103, 107, **137, 138**
*patte d'oie* 59, 81
Paulet, Sir William 44, 45
*Pelargoniums* 122
Pembroke, 4th Earl of 61
pennyroyal 28, 52, 117
Penrhyn Castle **155**
penstemon 128, **155**
peonies 126
perennials 111, 124, 126, 127-29
pergolas 101
petunia 123
photinia 117
pinks 117, 128-29
Pitmedden 72, 73, 90, **97**
planting plan 144-46
*Plant-lore and Garden-craft of Shakespeare* 88
Platter, Thomas 32, 33, 37
*Pleasure Reconciled to Virtue* 15
Pliny the Younger 27, 38, 43
Plymouth Barbican Association 92
*Polianthes* 'The Pearl' 132
Pompeii 38
poppies 123
Porcher, M. 49
potager 104, 111
Primaticcio, Francesco 36
privet 53, 56, 64, 117
*Proffitable Arte of Gardening* 37, 43, 45-47, 49
Pythagoras's theorem 151
Queen's Garden, Kew 90
Ravenna 20, 21, **12**
Reading University 92
Red Lodge, Bristol **46, 52**
Regent's Park, Avenue Gardens 84, **114-16**
Repton, Humphry 7
*Retir'd Gard'ner* 70, **90**
Rheims Cathedral 47
rhododendrons 148
Richmond Palace 29, 30-32, **27**

Ridgway, Christopher 82
right-angled triangle 151
*Robinia pseudoacacia* 116
Robinson, William 84, 88
Rogers, Fairman 92
Rohde, Eleanour Sinclair 46, 59, 62, 64
Romano-British art 20, 38
*Romneya coulteri* 101
rosemary 28, 33, 52, 53, 64, 114, 139, 148
roses 97, 101, 104, 106, 111, 124, 134-36, **132, 158, 159, 160**
Rousham House 130, **132**
*Royal Parks* 84
rue 28, 40, 54, 115
sage 52, 53, 116
Salisbury, Marchioness of 13, 61, 92, 97, 98, 101
*Salvia officinalis* 116
*Salvia x sylvestris* 'May Night' **152**
Salvin, Anthony 80
*Santolina* 101, 114, 115
*Satureja montana* 115
savory 61
Scotch thistle 101
Scott, Sir Walter 8
Sedding, John Dando 86
Semper, Gottfried 15
Serlio, Sebastiano 29, 48, **31**
Serres, Olivier de 62
Seton, Sir Alexander 73, 74
Shakespeare, William 54
Shakespeare's garden 88, **121**
shasta daisy 126
shells 107
Shetlands 17
*Short Instruction Verie Profitable…* 49, **61, 64**
Slezer 68
Smythson, Robert 44, 56
snowdrops 121
soft landscaping 106, 117
soil testing 148
soil types 147
Somerleyton 83
southernwood 40
Speed 36, 37
spring planting 119-22
St Fagan's Castle 90
St Mary's Church, Lambeth 61
Stafford knot 31, **28**
Stafford, Edward 30, 31, 32
St-Germain 62
stocks 28, 121
Stoke Edith 82, **110**
stone chippings 107
Stonehouse, Walter 62, 66, **79**
strapwork 48, 49, 61, 78, **45, 106**
*Suburban Gardener* 77, **104**
Sudeley Castle 139
Sumerian carving 15, 21, **5, 7**
summer bedding 122
summer planting 126-37
sundial 64, 66, **81**

sunflowers 139
Surflet, Richard 49, 52, 86
Surrey 36, 37
sweet pea 136
sweet rocket 124
Swift, Katherine 54, 57, 138, 153
Switzer, Stephen 7, 70, 71, 92
tarragon 28
Tempest, Sir Charles, 82
template 144, 145
*Teucrium* 116
*Théâtre d'Agriculture* 62
*Théâtre des Plans et Jardinages* 62
Theobalds 54, 56
*Theory and Practice of Gardening* 72,**93**
Theseus 15
Thomas, Inigo 86
Thornbury Castle 27, 30, 32, **28, 29**
thrift 61, 68, 88, 117

thyme 28, 40, 44, 45, 47, 52, 53, 61, 66, 117, 138
topiary 27, 33, 37, 38, 101, 103, 104, 107, 111, 116, 117, **152**
Tradescant 101
Tradescant, John the Elder 9, 61, 144
tradescantia 126
*Traité du Jardinage* 62
Tredegar House 70, 74, **89, 92**
tree poppy 101
Tree, Ronald and Nancy 92
trellis 27, 44, 60, 106
Trentham 78
Trevelyon, Thomas 48, 49
Triggs, Inigo 68, 74, 86
True Lovers Knott 66, 92, 112, 142- 43, 146, 153, **2**
Tudor Garden, Southampton 90, 101, 115, 144, **40, 143**

Tuileries 59, 62
tulips 65, 119, 155, **146, 147, 148**
turf seats 27, 106
Turner, William 38
*Tutte l'Opere d'Archittetura* **31**
Utens, Giusto 46, **21**
Vallery 29, 32, 46, **33**
Varro 43
Vasari 25
Vaux-le-Vicomte 68
vegetables 104
*Venus and Mars united by Love* 15, **3**
*Verbascum bombyciferum* 124
Verey, Rosemary 13, 90, 104, 112, 142, **140**
*Veronese* **3**
Versailles 68, 76, 88
*Victorian Gardens* 83
violas **147**

Virgin's bower 107
*Vitis vinifera* 'Purpurea' 107
Vitruvius 27
wall shrubs 106
wallflower 121
walls 106, 107, 108, **139**
Walpole, Horace 7
Washington, George 92
water features 108, 142
Watson, Anthony 37
wattle 24, 27, 106, **19**
weeds 149
Weller, Eleanor 92
Welsh Historic Gardens Trust 90
Whitehall 33, 36, **35**
*Wild Garden* 84
Wilkinson, Sir Gardner 79, **107**
William, King 68, 74
Williams, Clare 33

Willis, Peter 74
Wilton 59, 61, **74, 76**
Wimbledon 56
Winchester House 44, 45, **50**
Winchester, 14th Marquis of 86
Winchester, Marquis of *see* Paulet
window glazing 28, 29, 37, **43-45**
winter planting 111-17
winter savory 43, 44, 47, 115
Wise, Henry 70, **90**
Wolsey, Cardinal 29, 32, 33
Woodchester mosaics 20, 21, **13**
Woodford, Johnny **124**
woodruff 138
Worcester, Battle of 65, 66
Wyck 68
Wynde, John 30
Wyngaerde, Anthonis van 32, **38**
yew 77, 84, 86, 101, 117

## PHOTOGRAPHIC CREDITS

The authors and publishers are grateful to all those who supplied illustrative material for this book and gave permission for it to be reproduced. Unless listed here the illustrations were taken from the printed works as given in the captions.

Title-page, figure i, 1, 38, 40, 41 *bottom left*, 43 *bottom right*, 46, 52, 59, 65-67, 72, 78, 83, 85, 87-89, 92, 100, 112-114, 116, 118, 119, 121, 124-39, 141-63, 167: Jessica Smith

ii, iv, 60: by courtesy of the Marquess of Salisbury
iii: Museum of Garden History
3: Metropolitan Museum, New York
4, 35: The Royal Collection © Her Majesty the Queen
5, 7: Dominique Collon
6 and all diagrams, drawings and plans on pages140ff © Anne Jennings
8: Editions Houvet
9: Glasgow Museums, The Burrell Collection
10: MS Cotton Nero DIVf94v and 22, 24, 25, 26: By permission of the British Library
11: Trustees of National Museums of Scotland
14: Clive Hicks
15: Giraudon/Bridgeman Art Library, by permission of the Musées Royaux des Beaux-Arts de Belgique, Brussels
16: Bridgeman Art Library, by permission of the President and Fellows of Corpus Christi College, Oxford
17: Douce R.213, The Bodleian Library, University of Oxford
21: Scala/Museo di Firenze com'era, Florence

27: Fitzwilliam Museum, Cambridge
28, 97, 101, 103, 123: Robin Whalley
29: Thornbury Castle, Bristol
30, 33, 74 (courtesy of Worcester College, Oxford), 76: Conway Library, Courtauld Institute of Art
34, 55: Board of Trustees of the National Museums and Galleries of Merseyside (Walker Art Gallery, Liverpool)
36: Ashmolean Museum, Oxford
39: National Trust Photographic Library / Angelo Hornak
45, 106, 109, 110, 117, 122: Country Life Picture Library
50 a and b: Museum of London
53: The Warden and Fellows of All Souls College, Oxford
54 MS Cherry 36: The Bodleian Library, University of Oxford
75: Royal Borough of Hounslow
79: The President and Fellows of Magdalen College, Oxford
91: Witt Library, Courtauld Institue of Art
94 detail of John Gordon of Rothiemay's plan of Edinburgh, 1647: Courtesy of the Trustees of the National Library of Scotland
98: London Borough of Richmond upon Thames
99: William Page
105: National Trust
108: Royal Horticultural Society, Lindley Library
111: H.R.Tempest, Esq.
115: Public Record Office
120: The Pilgrim Press, Derby
140: Clive Nicholls
165, 166: Katherine Swift

## ACKNOWEDGEMENTS

**Robin Whalley**: I am grateful to many people who have helped with my research, but in particular I would like to thank Jane Avner, Angela Beazley, Andrew Dixey, Richard Fawcett, Andrew Foley, Michael Hunter, Caroline Kernan, Tony Mitchell, Keith Smith, Katherine Swift, Maurice Taylor, Michael Tooley, Rosemary Verey, Karin Walton and David Welch.

**Anne Jennings**: I would like to thank my family, friends and colleagues for their support and especially: David Beaumont, Elizabeth Brainbridge, Roseanne Flynne, Joy Larkcom, Paul Miles, Philip Norman, Mike Vandersluys and the gardeners at the Museum.

**Barn Elms** would like to add their thanks to Rosemary Nicholson and Phyllida Smeeton of the Museum of Garden History for embracing the idea of this book with such enthusiasm and to Sylvia Landsberg and Rosemary Verey for their help and advice. We are grateful to all those who generously allowed us to photograph their gardens and in particular: Richard Broyd, Mrs A. Georgiou, Bryan and Angela Hunt, Jo Rigby, Lord and Lady Saye and Sele, Christina Stapeley, Katherine Swift, Mr and Mrs H.R.Tempest and Mr and Mrs Michael Tollemache. We would also like to thank the following for their help with illustrations or other matters: Stephen Adams, Anthony Ashby, Mavis Batey, Sue Brown, Dominique Collon, Camilla Costello, John Crawley, Robin Darwall-Smith, Geraint Ellis, Geoffrey Fisher, Richard Flenley, Teresa Francis, Edward Gibbons, Julian Gibbs, Carolyn Hammond, Penelope Hobhouse, Elisabeth Ingles, David Jacques, Brian Jarvis, David Leigh, Clive Nicholls, William Page, Norma Potter, Shuna Rendel, Rosemary Smith, Jennifer Vine, Elisabeth Whittle, Kim Wilkie, Elizabeth Woodhouse and Jan Woudstra.

We are all indebted to Lady Salisbury for not only allowing us to photograph her garden at Hatfield, but also for so generously agreeing to write the Foreword to this book.